T0381068

Leadbetter's Possum
Bred To Be
Wild

Compiled by
Peter Preuss

From the diary of naturalist
Des Hackett

Order this book online at www.trafford.com
or email orders@trafford.com

Most Trafford titles are also available at major online book retailers.

Print information available on the last page.

ISBN: 978-1-4120-8382-9 (sc)
ISBN: 978-1-4122-0567-2 (e)

Trafford rev. 03/04/2019

 www.trafford.com

North America & international
toll-free: 1 888 232 4444 (USA & Canada)
fax: 812 355 4082

Leadbetter's Possum

Bred To Be

Wild

Compiled by
Peter Preuss

From the diary of naturalist
Des Hackett

Published by Peter Preuss, Melbourne, Australia

Contents

Acknowledgements

I WISH TO *thank Janet O'Shea, Owen Gooding and Jeanette McRae for proof reading the many versions of this book as it evolved, Marianne Hack for hour upon hour of typing and Andrew Batsch for the use of his splendid photographs.*

Photographs have also been provided by The Herald & Weekly Times Pty Ltd, Leader Community Newspapers Pty Ltd, Healesville Sanctuary and Don Willis.

Thank you to The Australian Wildlife Protection Council, Friends of the Leadbeater's Possum and The Upper Yarra Conservation Society for their endorsements and providing support in promoting this publication.

I also wish to thank the Yarra Ranges Shire Council and the Department of Sustainability and Environment's Community Forests Program *for financial assistance to layout, design and promote* Bred To Be Wild.

Finally, I wish to thank Ken Drechsler for his patience during the design and layout stages of this book.

Dedication

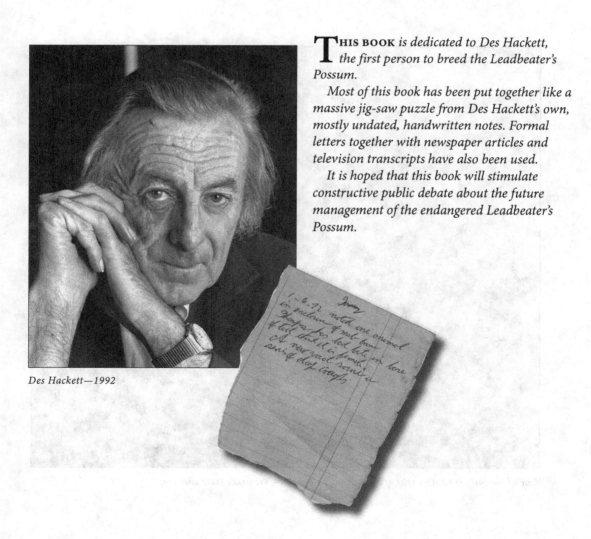

Des Hackett—1992

THIS BOOK *is dedicated to Des Hackett, the first person to breed the Leadbeater's Possum.*

Most of this book has been put together like a massive jig-saw puzzle from Des Hackett's own, mostly undated, handwritten notes. Formal letters together with newspaper articles and television transcripts have also been used.

It is hoped that this book will stimulate constructive public debate about the future management of the endangered Leadbeater's Possum.

One of the earliest photographs of a Leadbeater's Possum—Victoria's State emblem.

Introduction

THE LEADBEATER'S *Possum, or Gymnobelideus leadbeateri for those with a mind for Latin, would have to be one of the most majestic marsupials to ever grace our tree tops. It is little wonder then, that the Leadbeater's Possum is the mammal emblem of Victoria.*

Not seen for some fifty years prior to its rediscovery in 1961, this beautiful little possum was once considered to be extinct. It was however quickly found in many new locations thereafter and was initially believed to be on the increase.

The apparent recovery of the Leadbeater's Possum is believed to be in response to the extensive 1939 bushfires that swept through most of the Central Highland Forests of Victoria. Ironically, the very fires that almost pushed the species over the edge of extinction actually created the ideal habitat for this very specialised possum.

Prior to 1939 there were still vast stands of huge Mountain Ash trees within the natural range of the Leadbeater's Possum. After the fires, many of these trees were left standing as dead, and often hollow 'stag' trees. These stags together with the flush of thick regrowth that followed the fires created exactly what the Leadbeater's Possum needed. Essentially, there were plenty of nesting sites and a diverse range of food.

While the initial Leadbeater's 'fight-back from extinction' story is encouraging, the future of the Leadbeater's Possum is not necessarily a certainty. The species continues to have a very limited natural range and the stags left after the 1939 fires are gradually giving in to time and gravity. Current forest management practices are also frequently criticised for not accommodating the long-term needs of species such as the Leadbeater's Possum.

'Stags'—typical nesting trees for the Leadbeater's Possum.

A Very Political Animal

Unfortunately, most of the forests in which the Leadbeater's Possum can be found are potentially subject to clear-felling operations.

The timber industry quickly seized onto the perception that the Leadbeater's Possum were on the increase, equating the impact of bushfires with the effects of clear-felling. The example was repeatedly used in the mid 1970s during a Senate Inquiry into the woodchip industry by Mr A.G. Hanson, the then Acting Director General of the Forestry and Timber Bureau.

"You will find that if you never log the forest where the Leadbeater Possum is, the Leadbeater Possum will disappear. The habitat of the Leadbeater Possum is a forest of an age between 20 and 40 years. So if you never log it, you are very rapidly going to lose the possum."

In time, this very simplistic assessment was proven to be grossly inaccurate. It is now understood that a major requirement of the species is an abundance of large, old hollow trees for nesting sites— not something that features greatly in a clear-felled forest.

As more information about the Leadbeater's Possum has come to hand, the animal has become a 'trump card' for the environment movement. The very existence of the Leadbeater's Possum in a patch of forest has made many areas a 'no go zone' for the timber industry. This has prompted many environmentalists to search for colonies of the animal in the hope of protecting our native forests from clear-felling.

After a fire, many dead trees are left standing.

Much of Victoria's tall forests were burnt during the 1939 fires.

Present distribution of the Leadbeater's Possum.

In 1990 a massive road was carved through a known Leadbeater's Possum nesting site.

An Environmental Dilemma

The Leadbeater's Possum has become somewhat of a political football, potentially at its own expense in the long term.

Our zoos and sanctuaries have successfully bred the Leadbeater's Possum in captivity and there is a comprehensive state government management plan for the species. However, the Leadbeater's Possum remains one of Australia's most endangered mammals. How can this be?

While the timber industry chips away (excuse the pun), fear of excluding areas from harvesting may well remain the major reason why captive bred Leadbeater's Possum are not released into the wild. Yet, our zoos and sanctuaries have faced the dilemma of having surplus stock.

What follows is the story behind this dilemma. It is not an attempt to scientifically document the physiology or habitat requirements of this endangered species. Such a task is best left to university and wildlife authority biologists. Rather, what follows is a tribute to one man who was able to turn the tide of extinction for the Leadbeater's Possum. This is Des Hackett's story, the first man to breed the Leadbeater's Possum (and Sugar Gliders) in captivity.

About Des Hackett

I first met Des Hackett at his Blackburn home in the mid-1980s. A tall wooden fence separated his weatherboard house from the rest of the inner Melbourne suburb of neat gardens and cement driveways. He was a suburban hermit, a recluse, and he was clearly not fond of most other people.

To venture through his front gate was to enter another world. His home, on a typical suburban quarter acre block, was almost hidden among tall gums and shady ferns. The ground was thick with fallen logs and leaf litter.

Des Hackett's backyard was dominated by huge breeding cages.

Though quite young, this urban forest looked like it could have been a remnant of the original Blackburn forest prior to the area giving way to suburbia. Even the air was cool and smelt like a rainforest.

Many wild animals had made this garden their home. Ringtail Possum nests were scattered among the shrubs, while large Brushtailed Possums occupied the nesting boxes tied to trees. A multitude of birds frequented the yard, including the occasional owl.

It was the backyard that attracted the night hunters. Rows of huge cages dominated the yard. Each was richly supplied with branches, nesting boxes and freshly cut foliage.

It was in this very unusual backyard that Des Hackett had been breeding Sugar Gliders and Leadbeater's Possum.

I soon learnt that Des Hackett was a long-time environmental campaigner. He fought against the use of the hideous 'steel-jaw-leg-hold trap' and often exposed cruel and unsustainable activities within the kangaroo industry. He had recently helped establish a private sanctuary known as 'The Three Patriarchs' on Flinders Island specifically for the endangered Cape Barren Geese which were still being relentlessly hunted at the time.

Since 1980, Des Hackett had released hundreds of Sugar Gliders into areas where they had become locally extinct. Notably, follow-up research by the Victorian Fisheries and

The backyard attracted owls.

Wildlife Department had shown great success in recolonising the Tower Hill Reserve near Warrnambool with animals bred by Des Hackett.

Des was immensely proud of his contributions. He was particularly proud of contributing to our understanding of the Leadbeater's Possum. However, he was frustrated by the lack of political will to ensure the survival of this endangered animal.

Des Hackett campaigned against the steel jaw trap.

The Hackett Tree

Des Hackett's work with the Leadbeater's Possum was potentially his most significant work given the status and limited range of the animal. Almost nothing was known about the species prior to his efforts.

Over more than a decade, I got to know Des Hackett well. Unfortunately, I saw him become very bitter. He had worked tirelessly and successfully on a range of wildlife conservation issues, but the plight of the Leadbeater's Possum remained his priority.

Although he was the first to successfully breed the Leadbeater's Possum in captivity, providing zoos with their first breeding stock and the benefit of his hard earned knowledge, Des received little formal recognition.

He received even less say in the ultimate destiny of the animals that were bred by zoos. His dream of seeing captive-raised Leadbeater's Possum released into the wild became less and less likely as the years dragged on.

Des Hackett with volunteers building the Hackett Tree boardwalk—1990.

In 1991, Des was acknowledged for his efforts by several environment groups. They rallied together to construct a boardwalk to a huge Mountain Ash near Powelltown. Known as 'The Hackett Tree', this giant had survived the 1939 bushfires to become home to a colony of Leadbeater's Possum.

The construction of the boardwalk, viewing platform and information shelter involved hundreds of volunteers, many of them local to the area. One local saw-miller even donated the timber used for the project.

The Hackett Tree Project was designed to provide an opportunity for people to view the elusive Leadbeater's Possum in the wild and to educate people about the need for sustainability within the timber industry.

Unfortunately, just one month after the Hackett Tree Project was publicly launched, the tree was deliberately torched and the interpretive material within the shelter stolen. This act of vandalism probably killed the Leadbeater's Possum colony and almost destroyed the 400 year old Mountain Ash. Des Hackett was devastated.

A few years later, Des moved to Swan Hill were he died in August 1997. Only a few close friends attended his funeral service. A month later, a large number of people gathered at the Hackett Tree where a plaque was set beneath the old Mountain Ash in his memory.

A Tribute To Des Hackett

It was at Des Hackett's memorial service that one of his friends gave me a box that he had found while clearing out Des's home. It was marked 'Leadbeater's stuff for Peter' in Des's distinctive handwriting.

Almost eight years later, I completed the task of sifting through the box of documents. Some of what follows in this book comes from what was in neatly presented folders: dated, typed and photocopied letters. Most however, was in the form of undated handwritten notes, sometimes on the back of envelopes or whatever Des found handy at the time of his observations.

I have put together these notes, letters and newspaper clippings, into what I hope is a reasonable order. I have tried not to edit the

Des Hackett with one of his many Sugar Gliders.

contents so that what follows remains an honest account of the work, discoveries, feelings and views of Des Hackett.

In doing this, I discovered a dark side to Des Hackett, particularly during his early years of involvement with wildlife. How he first acquired an interest in Leadbeater's Possum was most surprising as I only gained his acquaintance much later.

For those that may take offence at the earlier entries to this 'diary', I urge patience. As you read on, you will find a man initially driven by curiosity evolve into a passionate man with the honest quest to save the Leadbeater's Possum from extinction.

1
Early Encounters

Q**UITE BY** *accident, Des Hackett found himself in possession of a pet Sugar Glider in 1965.*

Des knew little about wildlife at the time. However, having previous experience as a dog breeder, Des decided to find a mate for his pet glider. He began exploring the Victorian mountain forests near Noojee for other Sugar Gliders.

Instead of gliders, Des captured a family of animals that he could not identify. They turned out to be the endangered Leadbeater's Possum.

Believed to be extinct only a few years earlier, these Leadbeater's Possum were the first of their species in captivity.

Knowing that it was illegal to keep even Sugar Gliders in captivity without a permit, let alone Leadbeater's Possum, Des Hackett decided to keep his discovery a secret. He attempted to breed both Sugar Gliders and Leadbeater's in captivity without telling anyone about his work.

From the prolific notes of Des Hackett.

My First Sugar Glider—1965

IN MAY 1965, I met an old bushman with an odd pet. It was a Sugar Glider called Fred. I had never seen a Sugar Glider before.

He had found it as a baby in the pouch of its dead mother and had reared it into a beautiful pet. But he had to move into a flat and asked me to mind it.

I did not want to take it but the man said he would call for him later so I took it.

The animal was very attached to this man and the old bushman wept when he gave Fred to me.

I waited for this man to collect Fred, but I never saw him again.

It took three months for Fred to get used to me.

I found that very little was known about Sugar Gliders apart from what I could find in a book called *'Gliders of the Gum Trees'*.

In 1967, I was given a female Sugar Glider called Flossie from Castlemaine.

I managed to breed Fred and Flossie, thus starting a very successful breeding program. I discovered much about the social structure of the Sugar Glider, how they care for their young and their dietary requirements.

I have since released hundreds of Sugar Gliders into areas where they had become locally extinct, and have thus contributed to the future survival of the species. The Leadbeater's story is, however, a very different one.

In Search Of Another Glider

During 1966, I decided to talk to people living in the bush—farmers, mill workers, tree loppers etc. Some of these people had seen Sugar Gliders and promised to assist me in getting what I wanted—a mate for Fred.

But the weeks and months rolled by with no results. It just seemed impossible to capture a mate for my pet and I almost gave up hope.

One day in early February 1967, I was walking in the bush some twenty-five miles north-east of Noojee. Dusk was approaching when I saw two small animals running along a branch of a small tree. I had a good view of them and was quite sure that they were Sugar Gliders.

I returned to Melbourne and thought a lot about my sighting

of the two animals. I decided that if my little pet glider was ever to have a mate, a determined attempt must be made to locate the tree that these animals lived in.

With a friend and a chainsaw, I returned to where I had seen the animals. On the eighth of March 1967, we decided to fell all likely trees with hollows in them. We started closest to where the animals were seen and kept felling in ever widening circles.

By the time fourteen trees had fallen we were over a quarter of a mile from where the animals had been seen. As we had found nothing, we were becoming very discouraged.

Finally, we found a tree that was about two feet in thickness. Some eight feet above ground level was a small crack or slot. Something had been using this hollow tree. I was doubtful that it could be Sugar Gliders as the entrance seemed too narrow. The only way they could have entered would have been in a sideways manner.

None the less, the chainsaw was set in the tree about three feet from ground level. When the tree fell, it could be seen that the trunk was hollow. In the standing stump was a mass of fine stuff like wood shavings from which two grey animals jumped out onto the ground and raced off at great speed.

We chased them, but they got into thick undergrowth and we lost them.

Cursing, we returned to the stump. A head suddenly popped out of the shavings and ducked under again. I quickly put a log over the stump, put my hand in the nest and brought out four animals.

Not Gliders

Three of the animals were males. The fourth animal was a female with two mouse-size young in her pouch. These babies, one male and one female, were fully furred but their eyes were still only partly open.

One of the adult males was considerably larger than the other two. He appeared to be a much older animal but in excellent condition. I assumed he must have been the mate of the female and that the other two animals might have been their offspring.

To my great disappointment, I could see that these animals that looked like Sugar Gliders were not Sugar Gliders. I did not know what they were.

I was at the point of letting them go when I realised that their home had been destroyed and that the two babies would die. I decided to take them home to rear them.

I took what I could of the nest with me. It was made up of strips of bark, all inter-woven with the appearance of wood shavings.

I placed this nest and the animals into a wooden box, eighteen inches long, sixteen inches wide and ten inches deep. They spent the first night in this box.

During the night they tried to bite their way out. But the box was made of one inch thick pine. In spite of this thickness, they were able to bite half way through. In one more night, they would have easily eaten their way out.

In the morning, owing to their efforts to break out, the nest was badly broken up and one baby was out of the female's pouch. I held the mother and this baby got back into the pouch.

Back In Melbourne

I took the animals back to Melbourne the following morning.

In my backyard, under a gum tree, I had an enclosure ready for Sugar Gliders. It was twelve feet long, five feet wide and six foot high. In this enclosure, I had already placed a number of stringy-bark logs about sixteen inches in circumference. These logs were in upright, horizontal and sloping positions. I also placed fresh branches from a gum tree at one end of the enclosure.

I then placed a thick log, two feet and six inches in height, into a sheltered corner of the enclosure. This log weighed about sixty pounds and was not likely to move. On top of this log, I placed the box containing the animals and their nest.

As dusk approached, the first animal's head appeared at the entrance of the nesting box. It sniffed the air in all directions, then climbed out and leapt up onto a log. The other three quickly followed, each one repeating the procedure of the first.

They carefully, but quickly inspected the whole of the enclosure. Within half an hour the animals were completely familiar as to where the food and water containers were. They were all going in and out of the nest as if they had been doing so all their lives.

I fed these animals the same food as I had been feeding Fred the Sugar Glider, who at this stage was almost four years old. This consisted of raw tomato, sugar-water and condensed milk with some honey mixed in.

Whenever I walked near the enclosure, the animals all

followed me around by climbing along the wire of the enclosure. They tried to get as close to me as possible. They seemed devoid of fear.

Later that night, I entered the enclosure. To my astonishment, the animals climbed all over my body, sat on my shoulders, poked their noses in my ears and sat on top of my head. If I picked them up, they just said "tich, tich, tich…" This was the only sound I heard them utter.

This Was A Challenge

These animals were not Sugar Gliders. They looked like Sugar Gliders, but there was no flying membrane as in the Sugar Glider. They were also a good inch shorter than Sugar Gliders.

Unable to identify them, I contacted a friend who has considerable knowledge of marsupials the next day. He came and inspected the animals that night.

"Christ, Hackett!" he said. "These are Leadbeater's Possums."

During the next four weeks, I sought and read all the available literature on Leadbeater's Possum. It was scanty and minimal.

The animals as a species were named Leadbeater's Possum after the taxidermist at the National Museum, John Leadbeater. Also sometimes called the Fairy Possum, it is the state mammal emblem of Victoria.

To describe the Leadbeater's Possum one would say it is fifteen inches in length. It has a short dense fur that is grey or brownish grey on the back. It is a dull yellowish-grey on the underside.

The face of the Leadbeater's Possum is strikingly marked with black and white. A narrow black stripe extends from the forehead, down the middle of the back, to the base of the tail.

The tail is a distinct and peculiar shape and is densely furred. Near the body it is flattened and narrow, but it becomes more bushy towards the tip. It is used as a counter balance to the body's active movement.

The feet are also very distinctive, for each toe is a large fleshy pad designed for a non-slip grip on smooth branches.

Beyond this, very little was known about the Leadbeater's Possum as only five specimens had been acquired between the years 1867 and 1909.

The first two known specimens, thought to be a pair, came from somewhere near the Bass River in South Gippsland in 1867. At the time, this part of Victoria was still forested.

In 1909, a specimen came from Mt. Wills, 150 miles from Melbourne in the Highlands of Victoria. A gold miner had shot a small animal on the roof of his hut. He did not know what it was so he sent the skin to the Melbourne Museum where it was identified as a Leadbeater's Possum.

Nothing further was known of Leadbeater's Possum from then on. Unexpectedly, a colony was discovered near Marysville in 1961.

Until this discovery, the Leadbeater's Possum was believed to be extinct. As this was just a mere six years earlier, I realised that the animals I had in my possession were the only Leadbeater's Possum in captivity.

What should I have done with the animals? Should I have handed them over to the Victorian Wildlife Department? But how would I explain how I got them?

I decided that the scientist knew no more about the Leadbeater's Possum than I did. To me this was a challenge. I would keep the animals and try to breed them. I also decided to tell nobody that I had them.

2
Early Observations
1967–1968

FOR EIGHTEEN months, Des Hackett secretly kept the Leadbeater's Possum in large cages in his Blackburn backyard.

During this time, Des made many notes of his work and observations, mostly on scrap paper.

Des Hackett's initial efforts to breed the Leadbeater's Possum were unsuccessful. However, his observations and the conclusions he came to about the habitat requirements of the species later became extremely valuable in finding other wild populations.

Also during this time, Des came into possession of Sugar Gliders. These he did successfully breed.

As Des was such a prolific note-taker, he would have also documented his earlier work with Sugar Gliders. Unfortunately, there was little reference to Sugar Gliders in the box containing his notes about Leadbeater's. Perhaps there is another box somewhere containing Des's work with Sugar Gliders.

The Ballet Of The Possums

I SOMETIMES ILLUMINATED one end of the enclosure with a fifteen watt electric light. I could then sit back and watch a display of high speed, agile running and jumping which is impossible to observe in the bush. I call it the 'Ballet of the Possums'.

In movement, the Leadbeater's Possum are extremely agile, graceful and breathtakingly beautiful. They leap sideways, forwards, upwards and downwards with great speed.

Their favourite method of progress is that of jumping from limb to limb, bough to bough. They can jump five feet in distance at a time.

They run very swiftly along horizontal logs and can run just as fast along the underneath of a log in an upside down position. When running upside down, they will sometimes let go and while falling, roll over and land on their feet on a log below the one they were running on.

While they can run just as swiftly up a sloping log, they are not as fast moving when they climb an upright log. They will actually avoid climbing upright logs if possible.

The hindquarters of the Leadbeater's Possum are much more powerfully developed than the forequarters. When picked up, they will struggle in the same way as a rabbit, with all power in the hindquarters. It is surprising just how hard they are to hold, being much stronger than they look.

In movement, the Leadbeater's Possum is extemely agile.

When they leap, the hindquarters are the propellants and on landing the hind feet also touch first. When it suits them, they can jump slowly and at other times very fast. Frequently stopping, they also stand upright on their hind legs, looking all around. This upright stance is strikingly beautiful and they look just like a tiny kangaroo.

To watch them jumping from limb to limb, the animals look and give the impression that one is watching tiny rock wallabies.

To imagine a Leadbeater's Possum moving through the scrub in a hurry, just picture a tiny kangaroo hopping at great speed. Not on the ground, but from limb to limb in the scrub. This is the way Leadbeater's like to travel.

Of course the Leadbeater's do run along limbs and climb just like any other possum, but no other possum hops through the bush like the Leadbeater's. It can be seen from movement alone that the Leadbeater's Possum is not likely to be found in lightly timbered bush or sparse scrub.

A Sad Start

Some nights, upon leaving the nest, the female had both babies in the pouch. Most nights however, she left the babies in the nest. She was obviously able to take them out of the pouch when it suited her.

On March 17, I noticed one baby to be very weak. It died that night. Twenty four hours later, the other baby also died. I put the babies into a jar of meths.

Both babies had seemed well enough. So why did they die? I believe that they died of exposure. To begin with, the nest was all broken up and the box containing the nest was much too big for them to stay warm.

Some nights the babies would spend the whole night at one end of the box alone. When the four adults returned in the morning, they would often be together asleep while the babies were left very cold at the other end of the box.

The Female Gets Sick

About one week after the babies died, I noticed that the female was wet from the lower half of the stomach down towards her hindquarters. This wetness appeared to be urine.

When I picked her up in order to confirm what the cause of wetness was, she reacted savagely and bit my hand. At the same time she made the hissing "tich, tich, tich…" sound.

The next day, the wetness on her stomach extended up to her chest. She was now very savage to handle.

At dusk, she was last out of the nest. She drank a lot of water, ate very little food and hurried back to the nest and stayed there for the rest of the night.

By the fifth day, the wetness extended right up to the underneath part of her lower jaw. She was now very weak and would stagger out of the nest last, make her way slowly to the water container, drink a lot of water, eat nothing and slowly make her way back to the nest.

I did not take her to the veterinary surgeon as they know nothing about marsupials.

On the eighth day, her condition had become critical. I examined her closely and discovered that it was not urine causing the wetness, but fluid continually oozing from her nose. I thought she must have had pneumonia.

Ill and all as she was, at dusk she would laboriously climb out of the nest, make her way to the drinking container and drink a large amount of water. She displayed a tenacious will to live.

At about 12pm every night, I would open the nest and hold a small container of water to the sick female. She would immediately indulge in a long drink. At 8am every morning, I would repeat the procedure of opening the nest box and the female would drink more water.

Some days I would try to coax her to eat mealy grubs. Sometimes she would eat two or three.

For a while I was puzzled as to why the fluid from her nose should be all over the underside of her body. Then it dawned on me that she slept curled up in a ball with her nose tucked into her stomach. This is the way all Leadbeater's sleep.

The animal kept licking herself, trying to dry up the wetness. By the tenth day, the wetness had extended right down the inside of both hind legs and also the inside of both front paws.

By the fourteenth day, the fur had started to fall out around her stomach, chest and on the inside of all her legs. She was now skin and bones.

I still kept the water up to her, now three times a night. I also got her to eat one or two grubs while in the nest.

At the end of twenty-one days, all the fur from the tip of her lower jaw, down inside her front paws, down her chest, stomach and down the inside of her hind legs had fallen out. The whole of her underside was completely naked and I was astonished that she was still alive.

Recovery

Twenty-three days after the female first seemed ill, the fluid from her nose was no longer a continuous flow. It became a spasmodic flow. By the twenty-eighth day, the flow of fluid had ceased all together.

During this period, she lessened her intake of water and began to eat more grubs, white sugar, condensed milk and honey. She also spent about thirty minutes out of the nest at a time.

By the end of the fifth week, she had completely recovered and regained her appetite. Her fur had also started to grow again.

As to what the illness was, I do not know for sure. What saved her from dying was my giving her water to drink while she was in the nest, the warmth of the other three males, plus her inherent toughness.

I am sure that this illness would have proved fatal in the bush. She would have to leave the nest two or three times a night for water. In her weakened condition, she surely would have fallen prey to a predator.

Even if she survived predation, she would have died if she could not find water. If the nest was located high up in a tree, she would have been too weak to climb back.

Of course, the animal may not have even suffered this illness had I not taken her from the bush in the first place.

The All Important Nest

By April 1967, the Leadbeater's had been seven weeks in captivity. I made a new and slightly smaller box for their nest. This measured 14 inches in length, 10 inches wide and 10 inches deep.

I placed the old nest inside the new box. I then put this box and the animals inside a new and much larger enclosure measuring 30 feet long, 10 feet wide and 8 feet high.

There were well grown paper-bark shrubs inside this new enclosure. I also placed a number of stringy-bark logs inside the enclosure for the animals to run on, sit on and jump on. I had cut these logs from the Kinglake National Park.

On the first night in the new enclosure, I was surprised at the rapid way in which the animals investigated it. At the same time, they were always aware of the exact position of the nest. They could and did return to the nest at any time in a matter of seconds from the furthest end of the enclosure.

Several days after putting the animals into the new enclosure, I noticed one of the horizontal stringy-bark logs had pieces of bark hanging from the underneath side. On the floor underneath the log was a considerable quantity of bark. This bark consisted of the rough outer piece of the bark.

I opened the box containing the four Leadbeater's Possum and was amazed to see a lot of bark had been carried into the box. This bark had been inter-woven into the old original nest. The bark was specifically the inner bark of the stringy-bark log. It was fine and pliable and had been torn into strips about six to twelve inches long in a narrow ribbon-like manner.

Even of this inner bark, about fifty per cent had been rejected. Apparently, they are very selective as to what will be used in nest making.

Leadbeater's Possum carry bark with a loop in their tail.

Every night for several weeks, the stripping of the bark continued. The little fellows were flat out carrying bark to the nest using a loop in their tail.

On some days during this period, I would open the top of the box containing the nest to see how the nest building was proceeding. The amount of work and weaving that went into the nest was astonishing.

The nest was shaped like a large pear. The narrow end of the pear shaped nest had a small opening, being the start of a tunnel. This led into the large bulbous end of the nest which was a hollowed out chamber. This was the Leadbeater's sleeping quarters.

On the ceiling of this sleeping chamber was a small round opening used to regulate temperature. If the weather was very cold, the opening was closed or part closed according to the temperature in the nest.

On several occasions of a daytime, I opened this vent much wider than the Leadbeater's had it. One of the Leadbeater's would stand up on its hind legs inside the nest and with both paws, close the vent to the required size. At other times, I would close the vent completely. Then a Leadbeater's from within the chamber of the nest would open the vent.

For particularly cold conditions, the animals even kept a small bark ball in the chamber. This they pushed into the neck entrance, therebye keeping the nest at a desired temperature all the time.

After some weeks, the Leadbeater's ceased the stripping of bark from logs at this busy rate, but would add a bit more only from time to time. Every night though, the Leadbeater's worked on the nest. They altered it, reshaped it, reweaved the

Like this Sugar Glider, Leadbeater's Possum strip bark for their nest.

bark and kept the nest tidy, mainly using the bark that was carried into the box during the earlier weeks of frantic log stripping.

There can be no doubt that the two baby Leadbeater's Possum did die on account of the original nest being completely broken up and out of shape. When at night-time, the female Leadbeater's took the young out of her pouch before she herself left the nest, the babies could crawl all around the box containing the broken nest. The temperature would never have been constant.

In a properly constructed nest, the babies would have always remained in the bulbus chamber of the nest, snug and warm until the mother and other members of the family returned.

I soon found that the Leadbeater's always emerge from the nest well before dark. On cold, dull winter evenings, they often emerge from the nest as early as 3pm. On two occasions, I have even seen a Leadbeater's Possum leave the nest before midday in order to urinate. As they do this in captivity, I am sure they must also do this in the bush habitat in order to keep their nest clean.

Finding A Healthy Diet

During the first two days in captivity, I placed raw tomatoes in the enclosure and a mixture of honey and water (seventy per cent honey–thirty per cent water).

The tomatoes were partially eaten and about four tablespoons of the honey-water mixture was eaten. I also tried sunflower seeds which they would not eat.

On the sixth day, I tried white sugar moistened with water. This was greedily consumed.

After introducing them to sugar however, the Leadbeater's refused to eat the raw tomatoes.

I introduced live mealy worms to the Leadbeater's. They ate ten between them on the first night. The next night they ate sixteen. After about six weeks, they were eating about eighty mealy grubs every night.

In spite of eating all the mealy grubs, they also continued to eat plenty of sugar. However, the intake of honey-water was reduced to about one teaspoon between all four. Some nights, no honey-water was eaten at all.

When the Leadbeater's were eight weeks in captivity, I changed the diet. I stopped the honey-water mixture and stopped the sugar. I placed four tablespoons of undiluted sweetened condensed milk in a container. This was eaten almost at once. I also placed eighty mealy grubs in the enclosure as usual.

The condensed milk was preferred to the mealy grubs. They

It was important to find a healthy diet.

started to eat less and less mealy grubs. I increased the milk to six tablespoons per night. Consequently, they further reduced their intake of mealy grubs to about twenty each night between all four. The more milk I gave them, the less mealy grubs they would eat.

I soon discovered that Leadbeater's Possum are gluttonous eaters. On this diet, the males rapidly became very fat. The largest and oldest male, being very greedy and eating more than the others, put on more weight than the other two males.

Most of the excess fat built up on his stomach. The female, although a hearty eater (other than when she was ill), never put on fat like the males.

It became quite obvious that I was in real trouble with the Leadbeater's as regards to selecting a diet that would prevent them from putting on excessive fat.

I worked on a new diet. This consisted of fifty mealy worms every night and one raw tomato sliced in half with a very light sprinkling of white sugar. Twice a week, I gave the Leadbeater's four teaspoons of white sugar in a container moistened with water. Also twice a week, I gave them four teaspoons of honey and water mixture (seventy per cent honey–thirty per cent water). I gave them four teaspoons of condensed milk only once every ten days or so.

This diet prevented the males from getting too fat. While the oldest male did not gain any more weight, he did not lose any either. I believe he was eating more than his share.

Leadbeater's—The Hunter

Sometimes I would catch moths for the Leadbeater's Possum. These moths were greedily eaten. So were all types of wood grubs and most types of flying beetles. Slaters they would also eat at any time. However, they refused to eat crickets.

On the morning of April 14, 1968, I noticed an object lying on the floor of the Leadbeater's enclosure.

I entered the enclosure and picked it up. It was the hide of a mouse with only one front leg and one hind leg still attached. All the flesh, intestines and bones had been eaten. The skull had been broken open and its contents extracted.

How did this mouse enter the enclosure that was completely enclosed with fine wire? It was impossible for a mouse to get in. The mouse must have been caught while climbing on the outside of the wire from the inside of the enclosure by one of the

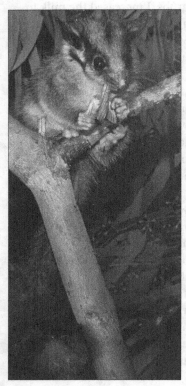

A Leadbeater's Possum enjoys eating a moth

Leadbeater's. The Leadbeater's must have then bitten pieces off the mouse until it was so reduced as to be dragged through the wire.

No doubt Leadbeater's Possum in the bush must also kill and eat small mammals and possibly birds. This is a reasonable assumption as these Leadbeater's were adults when taken into captivity and I often saw them catch insects as they flew through the enclosure on summer evenings. Allowing them to hunt in this way was important so that they could teach their offspring.

Other mice were often caught and eaten after that first one. I sometimes even bought mice at pet shops and put them in the Leadbeater's enclosure. They were quickly caught and eaten.

I often watched the Leadbeater's killing these mice. As soon as a Leadbeater's saw one, it would start to stalk it. Just like a cat, the Leadbeater's would move very slowly, and when a foot or so away from the mouse, the Leadbeater's Possum would make a flashing spring. They would grab the mouse by the back of the neck and kill it instantly by severing the spinal column.

Strangely, the Leadbeater's would not kill pure white mice. They would follow the white mice around the enclosure for a short while, then completely ignore them. I have the feeling that if a number of white mice were to move into a Leadbeater's nest, even these tough hunters would just leave the nest.

The Leadbeater's eat all grubs, moths and beetles by holding them in their forepaws while sitting in a semi-crouched or semi-upright position. The forepaws are used just like hands to hold their prey.

So in regard to diet, I discovered that the Leadbeater's Possum is very versatile. In my opinion they will, if hungry enough, eat almost anything. They are carnivores, nectarvores, insectivores and even tomato eaters. No doubt they eat berries in their bush habitat too.

I have also come to the conclusion that a variation in food is important to the well-being of the animal beyond diet. There is nothing more enjoyable than watching the little fellows eating a grub or moth and to note the great pleasure that they derive from these delicacies.

In captivity, Leadbeater's spend considerable time on the ground of their enclosure. They will pick up and eat food off the ground. I am sure that food would also be sought on the ground in their bush habitat.

The Leadbeater's Possum also drink a lot of water. On warm nights the four of them drank as much as ten tablespoons of water between them. Even in winter, each animal drinks at least one and a half tablespoons of water each night.

As the Leadbeater's tend to inject saliva into their water when they drink, it is most important to give them fresh water every day. Even one night without clean water will cause the animals distress. I believe that several days without water would result in death.

At certain times during the summer, there would be no dew on the trees and bushes of the Leadbeater's natural habitat. This makes me feel that the animal's natural nesting site would never be too far from a creek.

The Language Of The Leadbeater's Possum

Since being in captivity, the only vocal sound I had ever heard the Leadbeater's Possum make was a hissing "tich, tich, tich…." sound when I picked them up. However, on the evening of August 13, 1967, I made two very important discoveries.

On this night, I cut open a log for my fireplace. In the centre of the log were huge white grubs as long and thick as a man's thumb. I picked them up and went to the Leadbeater's enclosure. I held one grub in my fingers and placed it against the wire of the enclosure. All Leadbeater's came up and sniffed it. Suddenly, one grabbed the grub, raced off to a log, sat up and started to eat it.

The other Leadbeater's quickly descended upon the Leadbeater's with the grub and tried to take it off him. He resisted. Then a fierce fight broke out involving all four animals.

They fought each other by sitting on their hind-quarters, grabbing each other by the neck and head with their front paws. At the same time, the Leadbeater's relentlessly bit each other on the head and neck.

During this whole time, the animals were uttering angry high-pitched screeches, similar to rats fighting. It was a vocal sound that I had never heard the Leadbeater's make before.

The fighting stopped when I placed the rest of the big grubs into the enclosure. Peace was restored as each Leadbeater's was too busy eating what was obviously a real delicacy.

So, in spite of the Leadbeater's apparent gentle and peaceful nature, they will fight among themselves and they can make other vocal sounds apart from the "tich, tich, tich…" hissing sound.

Once, I left it rather late to feed the Leadbeater's Possum. On seeing me they began running quickly to and fro along a log near the food containers. One of them began to continuously repeat another new vocal sound that I had never heard. This sound started with a hiss and ended with a low moaning sound "ssss-ooooo, ssss-ooooo, sss-oooo..." In my opinion the meaning of this sound was that of impatience.

When I arrived home at about two a.m. one evening, the Leadbeater's were making a very low pitched rolling "r-r-r-r-r-r" noise, regularly repeated every ten seconds or so. In the morning I found an owl feather on top of the enclosure. I have thus concluded that this new sound is an alarm call.

Once, one of the animals had a bad bite on the base of its tail. It was making series of deep coughs. I assumed that this sound indicated pain or discomfort.

Further to a range of distinctive vocal sounds, I am certain that the Leadbeater's Possum is able to communicate with sounds that can not be heard by the human ear. After all, they do seem to respond to each other without seeming to make a sound and I have certainly seen them react to the soundless flapping of a moth's wing from a distance of twelve feet.

The Fearless Leadbeater's Possum?

If I left it late to feed the Sugar Gliders and Leadbeater's Possum, they had often already left the nest and were moving about the enclosures.

The Gliders always watched me from a distance. They remained cautious and only approached to eat after I had placed the food into their containers.

The Leadbeater's Possum on the other hand, would rush to the empty food vessels as soon as they saw me and began a frantic running to and fro. Every few seconds, they would pause to look into the containers. They showed no sign of caution and I often thought the Leadbeater's Possum to be somewhat stupid in this regard.

However, we have to be careful about assuming an animal to be stupid. It is not necessarily a sign of stupidity that the Leadbeater's do not recognise the danger posed by man, or dogs, or even cats for that matter. It simply means that due to the dense nature of their bush habitat, Leadbeater's have little experience of these potential enemies.

While I consider the Leadbeater's Possum to be fearless in many respects, I did make an interesting discovery on 27 August, 1967. I had placed a large branch of a gum tree into the Leadbeater's enclosure while they were asleep.

I had opened the enclosure, slowly pushed the branch into the enclosure, then got in myself, closing the door behind me. The box containing the nest of the sleeping possums was at the end of the enclosure, on top of a heavy upright log. I decided to place the gum tree branch in an upright position over the nesting box.

On moving, the branch made a continuous rustling and scrapping sound against the box. Suddenly, one after another all four Leadbeater's bolted out of the nest at an astonishing speed and in a great state of fright. They leapt and ran around the enclosure in all directions.

This event occurred in broad daylight and I believe that if they could have got out of the enclosure, the animals would have travelled a considerable distance before stopping.

To give some idea of the speed in which they quit the nest I watched one Leadbeater's Possum leave the nest opening, leap three feet up to a log on the wall of the enclosure and race along it for seven feet. When he came to the end of the enclosure, he turned left and raced a further five feet on a log before stopping. This distance seemed to be covered in a fraction of a second and he was so fast that my eyes could hardly follow him.

This was the first time that I had seen the Leadbeater's so panic stricken that they all left the nest in bright daylight. I have concluded that the intense rustling noise of the gum branch against the nest box had aroused a deep seated instinctive fear of some predator which makes a similar rustling noise.

I assume that it could be the goanna that stirs this fear within the Leadbeater's Possum as this predator is likely to make such a rustling sound while climbing. The goanna can get into hollow trees in search of prey, providing the entrance is large enough.

Goannas are a natural predator of the Leadbeater's Possum.

One calm night, I was observing the Leadbeater's as they were rocketing around their enclosure as usual. Suddenly, a small branch laden with gum nuts crashed down from a tree overhanging the enclosure. This sound and sight also terrified the Leadbeater's Possum, who immediately disappeared into their nest and stayed there for over half an hour. I believe that as falling trees can pose a real danger to animals in the bush, the Leadbeater's sought safety from this threat in their nest.

I have found the Leadbeater's to be thoroughly scared if their enclosure is illuminated with a very bright light of a night time. They will seek cover in the nest for quite some time before venturing out again after such an event.

My pet Sugar Glider hates the Leadbeater's. If I held him close to the Leadbeater's, they just clustered on the wire in a curious manner to sniff him. Sometimes the Sugar Glider would get very frustrated because I would not let him attack the Leadbeater's. He would utter a fierce grunt. This grunt also completely panicked the Leadbeater's and they would race and leap away in all directions.

In the bush, I am sure the Leadbeater's would give a family of Sugar Gliders a wide birth. If a family of Gliders decided to take over a nest tree of the Leadbeater's, I think they could do so.

Fire And The Leadbeater's Possum

On 14 April, 1968, I discovered the effect of smoke on the Leadbeater's Possum.

In a steel drum just several feet away from the Leadbeater's enclosure, I had placed gum leaves, men's socks, cotton singlets and pieces of sacking. I set the lot on fire.

The resulting smoke was great. The stench and irritation on my eyes and lungs were so bad that I could not stand it.

The Gliders panicked and tried to escape the smoke. The entire Leadbeater's enclosure was filled with smoke, yet the Leadbeater's would not leave the nest.

After twenty minutes, I removed the drum and put the smoke pot out in case the animals came to harm.

It appears that smoke will not make Leadbeater's Possum leave their nest. In the bush, I presume that smoke of a bushfire would also not cause them to flee the nest.

I believe that Leadbeater's Possum associates smoke with fire and no mater how great the smoke, they know that to quit the nest would endanger their lives during a bushfire (Gliders on the other hand may be able to move fast and far enough to escape a fire).

No doubt their lives are endangered regardless. However, as not all bushfires are the type that would completely incinerate the tree, nest and all, their chances of survival are much greater by remaining in the nest.

Death Of A Leadbeater's—October 1967

One night, I noticed that only three of the Leadbeater's Possum were out of the nest, running around the enclosure, feeding etc.

The one still in the nest was the largest and oldest male. He always stood out from the others on account of his size.

I had often noticed this large male and the female grooming each other and always assumed that they must have been mates. I believe the other two males were the sons of this male and the female.

In the morning, I entered the enclosure and examined him. He looked quite bright and normal. I thought he must have left the nest a lot later than the others. In other words, he might have just got out of bed later.

The following night, I again noticed only three Leadbeater's were out of the nest. The big male was missing again.

In the morning, I went into the enclosure and examined the big male again and could not see a thing wrong with him.

The following and third night he was again not out with the others. In the morning he was lying on the floor of the enclosure—dead.

The large male was always a gluttonous eater.

I examined him. There was no sign of injury on his body. So why did he die? He was a very greedy animal, always eating much more than the others. He was a gluttonous eater and rapidly became very fat in captivity.

I weighed him. The weight was six ounces.

In real life he looked beautiful. Such a magnificent animal was he that even in death he looked beautiful. He was a gem. I missed this animal very much.

I wrapped the dead male Leadbeater's up in paper, took him into the Melbourne Museum and left him there.

I told them that I had found this dead animal on the road in the Marysville area.

I did not leave my name and said that I was in a hurry but would ring back later.

In the afternoon, I did ring the museum and spoke to the curator of mammals. She said that the animal was a magnificent Leadbeater's Possum and was thrilled to receive such a specimen.

She asked other questions but I was evasive. I never trust women. Telling them anything is only a waste of time for they are incapable of putting to the best use any knowledge that is passed onto them. As it was, she did not know for at least one hour that it was a Leadbeater's Possum.

Fighting Among The Males

Male Sugar Gliders are all year round sniffing at the females and would, if the female permitted, copulate at any time of the year.

If male and female gliders are separated, the males will masturbate on a piece of fur, a piece of velvet and if allowed in the house, even expend their sexual ardour on mirrors.

In contrast, the Leadbeater's Possum show no such enthusiasm for sexual activities. In spite of the vast number of hours watching Leadbeater's, I had never seen the males show any sexual interest in the female. In fact, the males seemed quite sexless.

However, on the morning of January 29, 1968, I went into the Leadbeater's enclosure in order to remove the nesting box containing the Leadbeater's to another enclosure on account of a very hot day looming.

I was surprised to see a lot of fur on the floor of the enclosure. This could only have meant that there had been fighting.

I opened the nest and examined the animals. Both males had tufts of fur missing from various parts of their body—the fatter animal more so than the other. There was no other sign of injury.

That night, I watched the Leadbeater's Possum on and off for three hours. One male was limping but he did not seem distressed and could climb well. There was no sign of fighting. If

I discovered that the Leadbeater's Possum was a fighter.

there had have been, I would have removed one of the males.

I went to bed at about three am but was awoken by a thumping noise and a loud, continuously repeated, chattering sound. The disturbance was coming from the Leadbeater's enclosure.

I hurried out to the enclosure where both males were on the floor fighting fiercely.

I was about to enter the enclosure when one of the males broke away and ran along the floor to the furthest end of the enclosure. The other Leadbeater's Possum then climbed up a log, all the while closely watching the one on the floor.

Every now and then, the male on the log would race backwards and forwards on the log, the whole time making the loud chattering vocal sound. This chattering noise was so loud that it could be heard 100 feet away. It was no doubt a challenge to fight or a victory cry.

After about fifteen minutes, the male on the log, who was obviously the victor, dropped to the floor and rushed around and around the defeated animal. But he did not attack him. He returned to the log, repeating continuously his loud chattering cry.

Just before dawn, the victor again dropped from the log. This time he did attack the male on the floor. The defeated male barely defended himself. He was beaten and only wanted to escape out of the enclosure.

During the whole time this fighting was taking place, the female remained uninvolved in the nest.

The dominant male stopped fighting and entered the nest with the female. The defeated male then slowly climbed up a log and sat there until dawn. He then too entered the nest with the others.

After some time, I opened the box containing the nest and found all three Leadbeater's were curled up separately asleep. But at eight am, there was a scuffling noise in the nest. Then suddenly, in bright daylight, the defeated Leadbeater's Possum left the nest, climbed down to the floor, lay down, stretched his body straight out and closed his eyes.

I entered the enclosure and picked him up, whereupon he immediately bit my hand right to the bone.

I examined him carefully. He had tufts of fur missing from various parts of his body and several small skin lacerations on the head and body. None of the injuries however were deep enough to draw blood.

I placed the animal into a box, took him inside the house and gave him some water to drink. He drank a little, then tried to bite his way out of the box. He then lay down for about twenty minutes before making another attempt to bite his way out.

He kept up the procedure of getting up, trying to bite his way out, then lying down for a while. At noon, he lay down for the last time, closed his eyes and died at one-thirty p.m.

I froze the dead male Leadbeater's Possum and gave him to the Curator of Mammals at the Adelaide Museum on 21 March, 1968. I also gave him the two babies that I had kept in Methylated Spirits. He was highly delighted with such specimens, for the Museum had no Leadbeater's Possum in their collection.

I do not think that this Leadbeater's Possum died of injuries received in the fighting. He died because he was beaten in the fight over the female and he knew he had no standing in the nesting box. He was now an outcast and rejected. He died because he lost the will to live. There was nothing to live for.

If the fight had taken place in the bush, I believe that the defeated Leadbeater's may not necessarily have died. As soon as he was defeated, he would have run away and possibly have found a suitable tree in which to live. In time, he may even have found another female and thus begun another colony of his own.

The course of this fighting could only mean that the female had come into season. But, in spite of my knowledge of animals, I failed to grasp this until too late. Otherwise the animal would have been removed and he would not have died.

I learnt an important lesson from the fight. Male Leadbeater's Possum can be highly pugnacious and will kill each other in captivity when the female is in season. Leadbeater's Possum that are kept in captivity therefore must be paired off. There must only ever be one dominant adult male with one adult female. Single males and single females however may be kept together in one enclosure.

It is also interesting to note that both male Leadbeater's that have died did so out of the nest, obviously by choice. I believe that in their bush habitat this procedure must also be followed by dying Leadbeater's. Leaving the nest to die would be nature's way of preventing the nest from being fouled.

Leadbeater's Response To Hot Weather

Towards the end of February 1968, the temperature was around the century mark for days at a time. Then came a day when the temperature reached 106 (Fahrenheit).

On this day, the Leadbeater's were in an enclosure completely shaded by gum trees. Yet, the male left the nest in bright daylight and lay stretched out on a log. He remained completely awake. Until nightfall, the female Leadbeater's remained in the nest alone.

That night, it was very hot. In the morning at daybreak, the female was lying curled up half asleep on the floor of the enclosure, hidden under a gum branch. This time the male remained in the nesting box.

At about 1pm, when the temperature rose to 107, the male left the nest and lay stretched out, awake on a log as before.

I entered the enclosure and the male Leadbeater's Possum got off the log and entered the nest. When I left the enclosure, he came out again and lay down on his log.

I entered again and he did the same thing.

During the whole of this time, the female ignored me and stayed out of the nest until nightfall.

In the bush, very hot days must also compel the Leadbeater's to leave their nest and seek relief in some shady bush or even on the ground. No doubt they would remain awake or half wake as they did in the enclosure.

It is of interest to note that the extreme temperatures caused the Sugar Gliders to leave their nests also. In the same manner as the Leadbeater's Possum, they too stayed out of their nest, awake until temperatures dropped.

Leadbeater's Response To Cold Weather

The Leadbeater's are more active than Sugar Gliders, always leaving the nest much earlier. At dawn, while the Gliders are already in their nest asleep, the Leadbeater's are still out and moving about the enclosure.

Leadbeater's Possum also withstand greater extremes of weather. Bitter wind and heavy rain tends to keep the Gliders in their nest, but the Leadbeater's Possum will be out running around regardless.

On particularly cold nights, the Leadbeater's Possum may spend about twenty minutes at a time out of the nest, returning occasionally to the nest to warm up. They will stay out of the nest most of the night on very hot nights. Typically however, the Leadbeater's will leave the nest before dark, stay out of the nest for two hours at a time, return to the nest for a while and repeat the procedure all night long.

On Monday 21 April, 1968, the weather turned cold. That night the Leadbeater's began stripping a log and carting new bark into the nest for the first time in almost twelve months.

On this night, a female Sugar Glider that I had kept in captivity for five months also started breaking leaves off gum branches in her enclosure and putting them into her sleeping box. It seems that cold weather triggers off nest making activities in both species.

A Woollen Nest

During the winter of 1968, I cut a twelve inch by twelve inch piece out of a woollen pullover and placed it inside the Leadbeater's nest. This was rejected for sleeping on as I intended but the animals made use of it in a highly skilled manner.

Firstly, they dismantled one side of the bark nest and pushed the woollen piece of pullover outside the nest. The Leadbeater's then pulled the piece of wool right over the top of the nest. They then added many pieces of bark to the sides and top of the piece of wool, thus completely fixing it in position and making it part of their nest. All this work took two nights.

In making use of this foreign piece of material, the Leadbeater's Possum showed great skill and also, I believe, intelligence.

Regardless of this experiment, I am certain that Leadbeater's Possum can never be kept in captivity unless suitable bark logs are placed in the enclosure for the purposes of nest building. Log stripping for the nest is of primary importance to the Leadbeater's and no attempt to breed them will ever succeed unless this is fully realised.

Leadbeater's Without A Nest

One night I tried an experiment. I removed the nest from the enclosure of the Leadbeater's Possum while they were out.

The animals quickly knew that the nest was missing and became very disturbed. They searched the enclosure for it all night and as dawn approached they became quite frantic.

Suddenly, each animal selected a fork in a different shrub and curled tightly around it in a ball like position, then went to sleep.

When I entered the enclosure with the nest, the animals were asleep and ignored me.

I grasped one of the animals to put it into the nest and found that owing to the ball-like position, the animals were locked onto the branches. It was only after much tugging that each one could be pulled off the branches.

I noted that each animal had selected the best possible position as regards to protection within the whole enclosure. From this experiment we can assume that Leadbeater's Possum could survive some time without a nest. However, in the bush, I believe it will be found that the Leadbeater's Possum will only exist where there are dead and/or hollow trees as they need the nest for protection from the elements in the longer term.

The importance of the nest is understandable for the Leadbeater's Possum begins its life in the nest and will spend well over half of its life in the nest. It provides the animal with protection against the cold, heat, bushfire and predators. It can truly be said that a Leadbeater's Possum without its nest is like a fish without water.

Final Reflections

On September 1, 1970, I noted the female was drinking excessive amounts of water. Four days later, I found her lying dead on the ground of the enclosure.

During the last three days of her life she consumed 16 tablespoons of water. During this time she was active and showed no other signs of illness. She had been three years and six months in captivity and seemed to be an old animal. I believe that she died of old age.

A short time later, the last male Leadbeater's Possum died in a similar manner.

Over a period of three years, I was able to observe the beautiful Leadbeater's Possum in my own backyard. Though not successful in breeding the Leadbeater's, I had learnt a great deal about how they live and was sure that they could be bred.

I decided to contact the wildlife authorities in case there was anything they wished to ask me. I knew that this was risky given that I had no permit to keep wildlife. However, I had already been able to breed the Sugar Gliders and providing certain measures were taken, I knew that my experiences could help breed the Leadbeater's Possum too.

Des had successfully bred Sugar Gliders and was sure that his experience would help the Leadbeater's Possum.

3
A New Captive Colony
1971

D ES HACKETT *eventually made contact with the Victorian Wildlife Authorities.*

He was initially threatened with prosecution for keeping wildlife without a permit and even had to go to court. However, his success in breeding Sugar Gliders and experience in keeping the endangered Leadbeater's Possum was acknowledged.

Des found considerable support for his work from academics and staff within the Fisheries and Wildlife Department. Having the experience and facilities to breed Leadbeater's, Des Hackett was informally supplied with more animals. This included both Sugar Gliders and Leadbeater's Possum. He was also sometimes given injured Greater Gliders and Yellow-Bellied Gliders with the aim of rehabilitation for release into the wild.

By December 1971, Des had five Leadbeater's Possum in captivity. These he called The Gentleman, The Amazon, Tommy, Nixon (The Barbarian) and Mad Nora (later to be called Tessa).

Although he was never issued with an official permit to keep wildlife, Des Hackett was now determined to breed the Leadbeater's Possum and dedicated much of the rest of his life to this quest.

The New Leadbeater's

ON JULY 19, 1971, a research scientist from La Trobe University gave me a male Leadbeater's Possum. He had caught the animal in the Upper Thompson River area.

As he came from the Thompson, I named this Leadbeater's 'Tommy'. He was small in size and appeared to be a young immature animal. His belly fur was a pale grey.

I placed Tommy into an enclosure thirty feet long by eleven feet wide and eight feet high.

In the first week of August, I was given three more Leadbeater's—two males and one female. These were captured on Wild Dog Road in the Tommy's Bend area near Marysville. I placed these animals into the enclosure with Tommy.

I was initially threatened with prosecution for keeping wildlife without a permit.

One of the new males was a fully mature animal in his prime. He was a strong and muscular compared with the other males so I did not expect fighting between the males.

The fur on the belly of the big male was a yellow buff colour. I named him 'The Gentleman' as he was well mannered toward the other animals. When savage fighting did break out between the other animals, he remained aloof. Only on one occasion did he join in the fighting. He even seemed to put a stop to any squabbles between the other males.

The other new male was very small, probably only eight or nine months old. His belly fur was a pale grey. I named this animal 'Nixon' from the very start as he displayed a cocksureness and contempt for the other animals and always seemed to be the instigator of any trouble within the group. When they caught moths or beetles, he would snatch them out of their mouths and chase them away from the food container.

Nixon's behaviour towards the others was so outrageous that I regarded him to be a threat to the other animals. By September, I was calling him 'Nixon the Barbarian'.

The female, I named 'The Amazon' as she too could put up a good fight. She was fully grown, but young and immature, also with pale grey belly fur.

If possible, Tommy preferred to avoid fights. His nature was that of restraint. On occasions when he did fight, he proved to be a poor fighter.

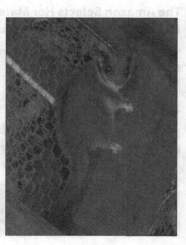

The Gentleman was forever trying to break out of the enclosure.

Efforts To Escape

Tommy, Nixon, The Amazon and The Gentleman did not settle well. Every night for eight weeks, all four animals made frantic attempts to break out of their enclosure.

All four Leadbeater's Possum selected and concentrated on one area of the enclosure—a damp section of ground. Sitting on their hindquarters, they would frantically scoop up the earth with their front paws, throwing the earth to the side or behind them. Their objective was to burrow underneath the wire netting of the enclosure.

Each night they managed to scoop out a trench three feet long to a depth of about four inches. But the netting extended a foot underground. Every day, I had to re-fill and pack down the trench that the Leadbeater's had scooped out.

I often watched the Leadbeater's during this labour. It was a pathetic sight as all four animals sat in a row digging at the earth with their forepaws seeking freedom.

I was however impressed by the fact that the Leadbeater's all selected the weakest part of the enclosure in their very determined attempt to break out. I believe that they displayed considerable intelligence in working together in this way.

The Gentleman also frequently employed another method to attain freedom. Pressing his head hard against the wire netting, his objective was to push the nails and staples out of the wooden beams. During these attempts, he would systematically and intelligently test every part of the enclosure over the course of a night.

While I felt sorry for these animals, I also felt that it was important to breed the Leadbeater's Possum in order that more be known about the species. The very survival of the Leadbeater's Possum may well depend on cruel experiments like this.

After two months, the animals abandoned further attempts to break out of the enclosure.

The Amazon Selects Her Mate

During November 1971, a new enclosure was built measuring

The Amazon and Tommy.

sixteen feet long, twelve feet wide and eight feet high. I placed Nixon (the Barbarian) and Tommy into this enclosure, leaving The Amazon and The Gentleman in the original enclosure. I hoped to reduce fighting between the animals and stimulate breeding between the pair.

About a week later, The Amazon began to behave in a very strange way. She remained at one end of the enclosure. Hour upon hour, she ran upside down on a ceiling beam for a distance of four feet, then on another beam for a further four feet, then another for four feet, then another. She was running continuously in a square, always in a clockwise direction.

She was still frantically behaving in this odd manner after three nights. I realized that she would have to be removed from the enclosure for she would surely die of exhaustion. However, I was unable to catch her at night.

The following morning, she even refused to enter the nesting box. I did manage to catch her during the day and that evening placed her into the enclosure with Nixon and Tommy. Her behaviour immediately became normal. That very first night I saw The Amazon and Tommy sitting together with their arms around each other. It seemed that The Amazon had selected her own mate.

The next night, The Gentleman who was on his own, became very upset and agitated. He ran around the enclosure all night long. In the morning he did not enter the sleeping box. He went to sleep under a log and stayed there all day.

I examined The Gentleman's nest box but could not find anything wrong with it. I feel that The Gentleman resented losing the company of The Amazon and must have been searching for her.

The next evening, The Gentleman emerged from underneath the log. He appeared calm and his behaviour was normal. In the morning he went to the nesting box to sleep as normal.

A New Female

Towards the end of December 1971, I was given another female Leadbeater's Possum. She had been picked up by a rally car driver in the Upper Thompson River area. I placed her in an enclosure with both The Gentleman and Nixon.

As dusk approached and the Leadbeater's left the nest, the new female began making a loud chattering noise. I called her 'Mad Nora' because she was so loud.

Clockwise from above: The Gentleman, Mad Nora, Nixon The Barbarian, The Amazon and Tommy.

Nixon the Barbarian followed Mad Nora around the enclosure making a clicking vocal sound. Occasionally, he would make a sudden rush at her ending in a short mock attack.

During this time, Tommy also began calling and chasing The Amazon around their enclosure, but without attacking her. Tommy seemed stimulated by the vocal calls of Nixon.

I now had five Leadbeater's Possum. The Amazon had

selected Tommy as her mate, and it seemed that Nixon the Barbarian and Mad Nora were also well suited. The Gentleman was now on his own.

(NB: In later notes, Des Hackett refers to fighting between the Leadbeater's Possum. It seems that he then paired The Amazon with The Gentleman and Tommy with Mad Nora whom he renamed Tessa. This left Nixon the Barbarian without a mate.)

Mad Nora and Nixon The Barbarian.

4
1970s—A Time Of Learning And Breeding

DES HACKETT *continued to observe the Leadbeater's Possum in his care for the next decade.*

He mixed and matched his small colony into pairs in order to breed them. Finally, in 1973, the Leadbeater's did produce young. Unfortunately, the first baby Leadbeater's Possums only grew to the size of mice before they died.

Suspecting a dietary deficiency, Des enlisted the help of the Werribee Veterinary Institute. A number of different diets were tried and Des eventually successfully bred and reared the Leadbeater's Possum.

During this time, Des also spent a great deal of time observing Leadbeater's Possum in the wild, particularly at one tree, later to be known as 'The Hackett Tree'. His observations of Leadbeater's, both in captivity and in the wild, greatly furthered our knowledge about the species.

Learning About Leadbeater's

IN THE early 1970s, I became a member of the Field Naturalists Club of Victoria and the Mammal Survey Group.

We met once a month and once every month we camped in the bush to take a detailed recorded survey of mammals in various areas. We did this by means of live traps and spotlights.

Our group numbered over forty and was composed of scientists, students, business men, teachers—all sorts—and of course we had permits from the Wildlife Department for this work.

In some parts of the Central Highland Forests of Victoria we discovered the Leadbeater's Possum to be quite abundant. We

Typical Leadbeater's Possum country.

counted eight Leadbeater's in two nights not far from Noojee and a total of fifteen animals in two nights in the Upper Thompson River area.

Prior to its rediscovery at Tommy's Bend near Marysville in 1961 by Wilkinson (a member of our group), the last specimen had come from Mt. Wills in 1909. It had been shot by a Mr A.G. Wilson—a miner working in the area.

Our group spent some time searching this area with no luck. I spent extra time in the Mt. Wills area and am certain that the Leadbeater's may still exist there. I was most impressed by the bush around Glen Wills, an old abandoned mining town several miles north of Mt Wills on the Omeo Road towards Mitta

Slowly recovering from the 1939 fires, Mt. Wills seemed good Leadbeater's habitat with nesting trees and wattle understorey.

Mitta. In my opinion, it is real Leadbeater's habitat—just the right type of scrub and bush. I am sure the Leadbeater's will be found there one day, and if not it would be a good place to release this endangered species if they could be bred in captivity.

I became particularly interested in the natural diet of the Leadbeater's Possum. Whenever possible I tried to observe them eating in the wild. This is not easy as the Leadbeater's Possum move so fast, are often high in the tree-tops and do not behave naturally when spotlighted.

During December 1972, a wattle tree in one of the Leadbeater's enclosures had the bark on the trunk and most of the branches heavily pitted by the animals. By January, these scars on the wattle tree began to exude gum. By the second week of January, this gum was quite plentiful and had solidified.

Over a period of a few nights, this gum disappeared. It was all eaten by the Leadbeater's. It would appear that the Leadbeater's deliberately chewed the bark to get the sap in the first place, and possibly to get the gum that followed several weeks later.

This observation may account for why the Leadbeater's Possum are most frequently found in areas where there is both an abundance of hollow trees and wattles. They need the old trees in which to nest in and I am sure that the wattles are an important component of a healthy diet.

The First Babies

One morning in December 1972, I saw something lying on the ground in the enclosure containing Tommy and Tessa (previously called Mad Nora). The thing on the ground was a baby Leadbeater's Possum—the first ever bred in captivity.

I entered the enclosure and found that the baby, though not moving, was still alive. There did not appear to be anything physically wrong with it so I put it into the nesting box.

This little baby Leadbeater's Possum was most definitely a male and although I did not expect him to live, I called him 'Tiny'.

One night during the middle of February 1973, I saw a very small Leadbeater's Possum moving around Tommy's and Tessa's enclosure. I was delighted that he had survived. For months I watched this animal closely but without ever picking it up.

At about 11pm on March 7, I noticed The Gentleman and The Amazon (now together in another enclosure) running around together. Something did not seem quite normal.

When I entered the enclosure and opened the nest box, a young animal from within the nest began calling. Both adults attacked me so I did not disturb the nest any further.

I saw the baby Leadbeater's for the first time at about 10pm on March 28. Riding on The Amazon's back, the baby was only about the size of a house mouse.

This baby Leadbeater's Possum died on Monday, April 22. It was still only the size of a mouse. Over a period of several weeks the baby had failed to grow. Why?

Meanwhile, I continued to watch the little Leadbeater's in Tommy and Tessa's enclosure. Finally in July, I caught this young animal and was astonished to see that it was a female. The baby male Leadbeater's that I had found on the ground in December was never seen again. It must have died. This female must have been it's twin. She was healthy and I named her 'Tara'.

In December 1973, Tommy and Tessa produced another set of twins. These were both males and I named them 'Tony' and 'Toby'.

The Amazon and The Gentleman also produced an offspring in December 1973. This was a female and I called her 'Nancy'.

Nixon Dies

At 6.30pm on March 9, 1974, I saw Nixon the Barbarian out of his nest trying to feed on honey. There was something obviously wrong with him.

I picked him up and he began gasping for air with his mouth wide open. Nixon died at 7pm that evening.

Nixon the Barbarian had been in captivity for two years and seven months. From the start he was too aggressive for his own good. I feel that his aggressive nature contributed to his early death.

As Nixon was kept apart from the other Leadbeater's for most of his time, he never sired any young.

Help From Werribee

Tommy and Tessa's boy twins both grew slowly for almost a year but seemed quite healthy until November, 1974. Then, Tony began to lose condition. He became very slow moving and inactive.

By the end of March 1975, Tony's condition had further deteriorated and he had the general appearance of being drugged or drunk with most movements lacking co-ordination.

During this period, the diet was seventy:thirty honey-water mix and tinned baby food (beef and vegetables or lamb and vegetables). Raw egg was added occasionally and meal worms were given two or three times a week.

I tried various diets and eventually settled for a honey-water mixture and field crickets only (my earlier Leadbeater's would not eat cricket). On this diet, Tony made a considerable recovery. There was a rapid gain in weight and an improvement in co-ordination. His movement improved to such an extent that he was almost normal.

At about 5pm on April 30, 1975 however, I observed Tony to be out of the nest. He was on the floor of the enclosure in a semi-comatose state.

I took Tony inside, placed him in a small box with a rubber hot water bottle. Within twenty minutes, Tony regained consciousness but became comatose again at 8.15pm. At 8.30pm Tony died.

On May 1, 1975, I packed Tony on ice and delivered him to the Werribee Veterinary Institute. I also gave them the bodies of Nixon the Barbarian and Fred, my very first Sugar Glider who also died at about that time.

A veterinary surgeon at the institute agreed to do post mortem examinations on the animals and agreed to pass the skulls and skins of the Leadbeater's together with the autopsy reports to the Fisheries and Wildlife Division.

It was with great interest that I read the detailed autopsy

Fred, the pet Sugar Glider, was twelve years old when he died.

reports from the Werribee Veterinary Institute. The animals had all died of heart failure due to white muscle disease resulting from the lack of Vitamin E.

This was obviously of great concern to me as it seemed likely that all the animals in my care might have been affected.

I found it puzzling that Fred the Sugar Glider had a dietary problem of long standing. He was twelve years old and unlike the other animals that I had, he was a pet. Consequently, he had an extremely varied diet all his life. For the first twelve months or so of his life Fred had been raised by an old bushman. So I can not account for his diet during those early months. Perhaps it was somehow inadequate at the time and the effect only realised much later.

Tommy

On 19 April 1975, I noticed that Tommy was moving very slowly around his enclosure.

Tommy was the first Leadbeater's Possum captured in the Upper Thompson River area in July 1971. He was also the first Leadbeater's Possum to sire young in captivity. For this he was obviously very special.

An examination of Tommy revealed a scab of congealed blood three quarters of an inch long on the back of his neck close to the head.

This injury could only have been inflicted by Tessa and/or their son Toby. I removed Tommy and placed him in his own enclosure so that I could observe and handle him better.

Tommy had been badly beaten up once before. Shortly after I tried to mate him with The Amazon in 1971, she attacked him. As a result of this earlier beating, Tommy never seemed to fully recover. His fur always presented a dull appearance with no sheen. He always appeared underweight compared to other Leadbeater's and he often looked scruffy. None-the-less, he had sired two sets of twins to Tessa.

On this occasion, Tommy became very slow of movement after the beating. He was also quite clumsy when jumping. His behaviour was similar to that of his son Tony before he died of heart failure. Naturally I was concerned.

I again consulted with the Werribee Veterinary Institute who suggested that a urine test would tell if Tommy also had White Muscle Disease.

On 13 May 1975, I tested fresh urine from Tommy and the

result proved positive. A moderate-to-large amount of blood was shown to be present in the urine. It had to be assumed that Tommy also had the disease.

Upon the advice of the institute, I included Vitamin E oil drops mixed with sugar into Tommy's diet. The diet was also high in protein with live mealy worms, live moths and field crickets. He also got honey.

This treatment immediately stabilised the disease and Tommy was soon in good health. Even his fur improved. A Sugar Glider with the disease was likewise treated and lived for several years later.

For the rest of his life, Tommy remained in good health on this diet except for an extraordinary physiological change. During his six years in captivity, Tommy had sired a total of four young. While two of his male offspring had died, another male and a female were very healthy. But then, in October 1975, Tommy's testicles became smaller.

Over a period of several weeks, Tommy's testicles vanished totally. At the same time, a pouch-like opening appeared in the very same area as that of a female's pouch.

In April 1977, Tommy began to lose weight again. Within a few weeks he began to continually pass urine and eventually had no control of his bladder at all.

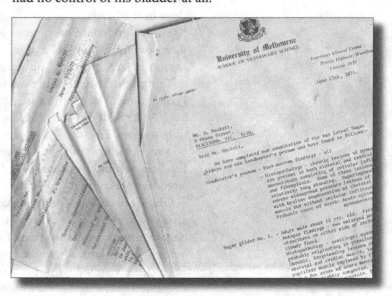

Autopsy reports from Werribee.

On May 5, 1977, Tommy became totally paralysed and I destroyed him with ether the next day.

On 10 May 1977, I took Tommy to the Werribee Veterinary Institute and gave instruction that a post-mortem report be forwarded to the Fisheries and Wildlife Department.

Problems With Particleboard

At dusk on June 29, 1975, I saw The Amazon and her daughter Nancy walking around on the logs in their enclosure. Both animals were staggering and swaying in a drunken-like manner.

I had observed the animals in their enclosure for some time during the previous night. They were out and about as usual and their behaviour was normal. This was too sudden for White Muscle Disease.

Both Leadbeater's staggered to the bowl that contained a honey/water mix and attempted to feed. Both Leadbeater's fell into the honey resulting in their heads and upper half of their bodies being drenched. Both animals were finding it difficult to breathe. Nancy was in a worse state, but it was clear that both she and The Amazon were seriously ill.

I entered the enclosure and looked for clues to account for the sudden illness. I opened the nesting box to find that there was an over-powering stench of foul air in the box.

Upon closer examination, I found a green fungal growth on the interior wall of the nesting box. There was also a vast amount of stringy-bark recently added as the animals had been busy collecting bark for the past six weeks.

I noted that the nest consisted of an upper and lower chamber connected by two tunnels. The upper chamber was still warm suggesting that the Leadbeater's had been sleeping in it.

The nest box was made of particleboard—a cube with a round hole for an entrance. I concluded that the large amount of bark had prevented effective ventilation. This together with moisture from the bark resulted in a poisonous combination. I think if the animals had been sleeping in the lower chamber rather than the upper chamber, they would have died.

It was not until about 2am that The Amazon and Nancy showed signs of improvement. They did not fully recover for a whole three days.

Clearly, particleboard should never be used for the construction of nesting boxes. As many people release wildlife, particularly after rehabilitation, with particleboard nesting boxes, it should be publicised that this is a very dangerous practice.

Possum boxes must never be made from particle board.

Toby And Nancy Mate

As soon as he was old enough, I put Toby (son of Tommy and Tessa) into the enclosure holding The Amazon and her daughter Nancy. I had already removed The Gentleman as The Amazon had shown considerable aggression toward him.

The three animals carefully smelt each other all over, then all went into the nest box together. They emerged from the box about half an hour later.

I was concerned about The Amazon's attitude toward Toby as she was the best of fighters. But everything looked peaceful.

At about 4.30am on the third night however, The Amazon did attack Toby as predicted.

Toby was no match for The Amazon in fighting. The Amazon kept running swiftly in pursuit of Toby. She would catch him, bite him, and pull out large amounts of fur. It was obvious to me that The Amazon intended to kill Toby, so I removed him from the enclosure.

I permitted a week to pass so that Toby could fully recover from his battering. I then removed The Amazon from the enclosure, leaving Nancy on her own.

I placed Toby into the enclosure with Nancy during the next night. Immediately both animals became friendly toward each other. They sat close together on a log and stroked each other with their forepaws.

During the next few nights I observed Nancy and Toby closely. They would often nibble the base of each other's tail. I believe this to be a sign of affection between Leadbeater's Possum. Toby and Nancy became mates.

Separating The Amazon from her daughter however, affected her mentally. She lost appetite, ate very little and sat for long periods in a moody state. It was obvious that The Amazon was fretting badly for her daughter.

Nancy on the other hand never looked back. She began taking bark into the nesting box almost straight away in the company of her new mate. From this experience, and others since, I have come to believe that the female Leadbeater's Possum selects the male as a mate.

The Perfect Pair

The Gentleman and Tessa (initially called Mad Nora) were paired up during the winter of 1976. They were well suited and I often saw them with their forepaws around each other.

They also affectionately nibbled each other's tail quite frequently.

Between December 1976 and February 1980, The Gentleman and Tessa produced a total of thirteen offspring—nine females and four males.

One female was taken to Monash University. This animal died within six weeks. They just did not know how to care for Leadbeater's Possum.

One male did die on my premises at two years of age. The others however all lived and grew well under my care.

In September 1981, I weighed The Gentleman, Tessa and all of their sons and daughters, except for one female which I simply could not catch. The Gentleman weighed 134 grams while Tessa weighed 138 grams. All offspring were heavier than their parents with males weighing 158 grams, 180 grams and 198 grams. The seven females weighed between 140 and 198 grams, with the average weight being 163 grams.

I had clearly developed a good formulae for the breeding of Leadbeater's Possum.

Tessa and The Gentleman ceased breeding in February 1980. While I think Tessa was still capable of breeding, it would appear that The Gentleman was beyond it.

In early May 1982, The Gentleman was still strong, eating well and running around the enclosure. Over the next few weeks however, he became slow and obviously weak.

Given that The Gentleman was already three or four years old at the time of capture in 1971, he may have been fifteen years old. He died of extreme old age at 10am on 27 May, 1982.

Goodbye old Friend.

Tessa and The Gentleman were very attached to each other and she badly missed The Gentleman. She searched for him for days after his death.

Soon after The Gentleman died, Tessa's eyes began to change to an opaque white colour. By August, Tessa seemed partly blind and she began to lose weight.

Tessa became very slow of movement and by August was very weak. On August 26, Tessa went into a semi-comatose state and died on 27 August, 1982.

I will always remember you Tessa—Goodbye.

Leadbeater's Hate Disturbance

On May 2, 1977, I placed the nest box containing The Gentleman, Tessa and two of their offspring (Gus and Gertie) into a small enclosure in my garage. A Monash University Research student doing a PhD on the Leadbeater's Possum wanted to inspect, weigh and measure my possums.

We noticed that Tessa had a tiny bean-like baby in her pouch. We wanted to study the baby but as Tessa struggled too much and as we did not want to distress her, we were unable to complete the examination.

At about 5.30pm, I returned the nest box to their outside enclosure. I inspected the enclosure again at about 7pm to find that Gus and Gertie were both missing.

I checked the enclosure in the garage again and found them running around on logs. It was obvious that they did not re-enter the nest box after being handled and had hidden under a mass of fern fronds on the floor of the garage enclosure.

When I caught and placed Gus and Gertie back into the outside enclosure with their parents, The Gentleman very carefully smelt Gus all over for about 15 minutes. It seems The Gentleman was making sure of the young male's identity. During this whole time, Gus kept making a vocal chattering sound.

I inspected the nest box and found it to be in a minor state of disturbance, the nest being broken open in some areas. The Gentleman appeared to be disturbed and agitated about the interference to his nest and kept going in and out of the box.

The next day, The Gentleman began stripping bark from logs in the enclosure and carried the strips of bark back to the nest box. Within just two nights, The Gentleman repaired the nest completely.

The research student returned to my home on the evening of May 11. Again we caught the animals. We found that Tessa's blind and naked baby, though still attached to the teat, could now move very actively in the pouch.

When I placed Tess back into the nest box, The Gentleman attacked my gloved hand, hanging on and biting. He was very agitated.

Two weeks later (May 26), we opened Tessa's pouch again. This time we could see that the naked baby was no longer attached to the teat. It was able to move its head in an active manner, but appeared not to have grown at all during the past week. Again, The Gentleman attacked me when I returned Tessa to the nest box.

A few days later, I saw a pile of bark that had been stripped from logs in the enclosure. This bark was heaped up in a secluded area of the enclosure and I believe The Gentleman was seeking a new place to build another nest.

This was the third separate occasion within five years that The Gentleman had built a new nest. Each time he built a new nest it was shortly after disturbance of the existing nest. Every time The Gentleman built a new nest, the animals always quit the old nest.

Clearly Leadbeater's Possum resent disturbance to their nest. In the wild I am sure that Leadbeater's Possum will try to relocate if they perceive a threat.

Sugar Gliders Keep Warmer Nests

May 31, 1977, was the coldest May day in eighty-five years. The outside temperature was only fouty degrees (Fahrenheit) at 5.30pm.

After The Gentleman, Tessa and the two young animals had left the nest for about ten minutes, I decided to risk further disturbance of the nest to measure the temperature inside. It was still fifty degrees (Fahrenheit) inside the sleeping chamber.

For comparison, I hunted a family of ten Sugar Gliders out of their nest, waited ten minutes and measured the temperature to be sixty degrees.

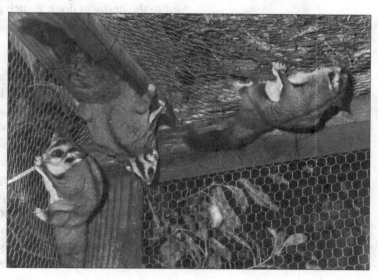

Sugar Gliders flushed from their nest.

It seems that Sugar Gliders are able to maintain a warmer nest than Leadbeater's Possum. This may be because of their size and/or their numbers as gliders tend to form larger family groups.

Nest Building After Disturbance

On 8 June, the research student again came to my home. When we opened Tessa's pouch again, we found that the young one had changed from a pink to dark colour. It was now growing fur.

At about 11pm that night, all four animals began nest building again. Tessa and The Gentleman were taking bark to the nest box while Gus and Gertie began taking bark to the top of some logs in one corner of the enclosure.

I placed a new box in the corner for the young animals but they stopped building this new nest and joined their parents in the main nest.

Be it because of colder weather or because of the disturbances, Toby and Nancy also began nest building in another enclosure.

For more than a month, all Leadbeater's made themselves very busy nest building. Balancing on their hind legs, the Leadbeater's stripped bark with their forepaws. They would pass the bark under their stomachs and grasp it with one hindpaw. Then balancing on the log with their forepaws, they would use both hind-paws to place the stripped bark into the loop in their tail.

Several pieces of bark would typically be stripped and placed into the looped tail before the animal hurried off to their nest.

This stripping of bark, placing it into the tail loop and rushing off to the nest was done at such great speed that it was difficult to follow with the eye.

Abandoning The Nest

Things were settling down on the nest building front when the research student came to weigh the Leadbeater's again on 13 July. All the animals except for The Gentleman freely left the nest when probed inside. The old man however refused to leave and attacked my hand, hissing and biting fiercely.

When we weighed The Gentleman we found that he had lost a lot of weight. Tessa's pouch young on the other hand had grown considerably and was now fully furred. It sometimes even hung out of Tessa's pouch as she moved around the enclosure.

Later, Tessa seemed quite disturbed by the handling and hid in the box that I had placed in the enclosure several weeks earlier for Gus and Gertie. Inside this box were now great quantities of bark.

For the rest of the night, all Leadbeater's worked at great speed to establish a new nest in an obvious state of agitation. It was clear that they would now abandon the old nest.

Toby and Nancy also abandoned their nest. They did not have another box in their enclosure. They made a nest like that of a Ringtail Possum dray on top of a log covered in gum branches in the most sheltered area of the enclosure.

Saying No To Scientific Curiosity

I was now convinced that disturbing the nest was not a good idea.

When the researcher returned again on August 3, I placed The Gentleman, Tessa and the two young adults into the garage enclosure while they were still in the box containing their new nest. We waited until all four animals had left the nest before removing the nest box from the enclosure.

When weighed, The Gentleman proved to have regained the weight he had lost three weeks earlier. Tests showed that he had no trace of Vitamin E deficiency. The loss of weight must have been due to stress.

To avoid unnecessary disturbance, I had taken the nest box into the house and insisted that this nest should not be touched. However, Tessa did not have the young in her pouch.

As we could not be sure if her young was dead or alive, I took a piece of wire and began probing the nest. Suddenly there was a scuffling noise which meant that the baby was alive in the nest.

The researcher wanted to open the nest in order to examine the baby. I was certain that such disturbance would result in the animals abandoning this nest again so I refused to allow it.

A Camera Shy Baby

Over the next few weeks, the baby Leadbeater's Possum joined The Gentleman, Tessa and the other two sub-adults in running around the enclosure.

I often saw the small animal running around but it always tried to hide behind logs. It was very shy and I could not tell its sex.

By the time it was half grown it could run and climb very fast, but I noticed that its tail was not very fluffy.

On 11 August, I tried to take a photograph of the young Leadbeater's Possum but it ran back into the box and refused to come out. I even placed food containers close to the nest box so that the youngster would have food close by. It refused to come out whenever I was ready with the camera.

It was quite some time before I could determine that this baby was a girl. I called her Gail.

New Genetic Stock

A male Leadbeater's Possum was captured at the Camberville Junction in June 1977 by the Monash University student. This possum, only known as Leadbeater's No. 16, was kept at Monash University until September 1979. He was then given to me.

Leadbeater's No.16 was at least six years old when he was captured. During captivity at Monash University, he was always a good size, weighing about 189 grams.

Soon after being relocated to my premises however, Leadbeater's No.16 began losing weight. He was never a healthy animal and he never bred. Perhaps if he had been given to me earlier he may have bred. I would at least have been able to try as I had female Leadbeater's Possum—something Monash did not.

On June 5, 1981 (*World Environment Day*), I found Leadbeater's No 16 curled up on the ground in a semi-comatose state. Sure that he would not recover, I destroyed him with ether.

In 1979, another male Leadbeater's was captured by the PhD students in the Camberville Junction area. This Leadbeater's was given to me and I named the animal 'Andy' after the research student who caught it.

Andy was about eighteen months old at the time of capture and already weighed 140 grams. He was big framed and by June 1980 weighed 180 grams.

I mated Andy with The Amazon, with whom he sired a female named 'Kelly' in December 1980.

Tessa Has Twins And The Amazon Gives Birth

On 13 September 1977, the research student from Monash University came again. He inspected Tessa and found twins in her pouch. These twins seemed to be growing well.

The Amazon also had one tiny young that had been born very recently. She had lost considerable weight but seemed to be well.

Some months earlier I had placed The Old Amazon in the garage enclosure with the young male called Gus. He was born to The Gentleman and Tessa in the spring of 1976 with a female twin—Gertie.

When I first introduced The Old Amazon and Gus, she sniffed

the enclosure all over. Gus just watched her closely from a distance. He seemed scared and did not know what to do.

After about twenty minutes, The Old Amazon approached and sniffed the young male. He turned and lay on his back while she sniffed him all over. She then performed the peculiar act of affection—nibbling his tail about an inch from the base. It seemed that two and a half years of loneliness had got the better of The Amazon's fierce nature and she took a liking to Gus. It was now also clear that they mated.

On 29 September, we examined the animals again. Tessa's twins were growing well. While The Amazon had lost further weight, her baby was also growing well. Gus had also lost ten grams. The Old Gentleman however, looked very good.

It was around about this time that I handed over the first group of ten Sugar Gliders to Monash University. There were six females and four males in the colony.

The University had also recently caught more Leadbeater's and I also saw a pair of captive Leadbeater's Possum being kept at Monash—a big male (180 gram) and a small female that I would say was only about one year old.

Gus Dies Suddenly

On the evening of January 4, 1978, I found Gus dead. He was lying in the water container and appeared to have been dead for twenty-four hours when I found him.

He had been in good health other than losing weight since being mated with The Amazon. There was no reason that he should die.

However, Gus was the swiftest moving Leadbeater's Possum I have ever had. On two occasions I had seen him misjudge his leaps around the enclosure after I had rearranged the logs within. Perhaps, while running and leaping around, he badly injured himself.

The Amazon was most upset at the death of Gus. She wandered around the enclosure searching for him for several nights.

I learnt that it is crucial to watch weight loss in captive Leadbeater's.

Tessa Evicts Her Daughter

At about 6am on January 5, 1978, I heard loud chattering coming from the enclosure housing The Gentleman, his mate

Tessa and their family. This meant fighting had broken out within the colony.

Upon inspection I found Tessa attacking the young female Gail. The Gentleman took no part in the fight and Gertie, the oldest daughter was also not involved.

I realised that Tessa had decided to ban Gail from the colony. As this matter is irreversible, I removed Gail to another enclosure.

By this stage, Monash University had realised that their pair of Leadbeater's were not getting on. The large male was beating up the small young female and they had been separated. Therefore, on January 10, I gave Gail to Monash University to pair up with the big male.

It was agreed that Gail would be closely monitored and that she be returned to me if she lost weight.

I also handed over the frozen body of Gus for research purposes.

The Amazon's Baby—Sahra

When the researcher came to collect Gail, we examined some of the other animals again.

Tessa's twins were growing rapidly. The Amazon however, could not be examined. About one week before Gus died, she had begun stripping bark to build a new nest in gum foliage around a log.

I knew she was still living in the proper nest box on January 7, but had since abandoned it. I also knew that The Amazon was still carrying the young in her pouch, so I refused to disturb her any further.

On the night of 14 January, 1978, The Amazon was running around her enclosure. I probed the new nest with a stick. The growl that came from within was the vocal call of a baby Leadbeater's.

On January 18, I again probed the foliage of the new nest. This time there was no sound. I then probed the big nest in the box with a stick and the baby Leadbeater's responded immediately. It was clear that The Amazon had taken her young back to the old nest in response to my probing.

The growling sound of the baby Leadbeater's had The Amazon running around the enclosure in a very disturbed state. She clearly resented the further intrusion.

On 24 January, I again probed The Amazon's nest. There was no vocal sound to be heard from the box. When I then probed the nest in the foliage, the young Leadbeater's growled. Then to my surprise, it ran out of the nest and climbed onto a branch.

I picked it up. It was a female and already quite large in size, about one and a half times the size of a house mouse. The Amazon had clearly done a great job as a single mum. She confirmed my belief that Leadbeater's Possum in the wild will move homes if disturbed or threatened.

Tessa's Babies

On August 15, 1978, it was found that Tessa had two tiny babies in her pouch. Reluctant to over-handle her, I never fully examined these babies.

On 8 November, I probed Tessa's nest box and a young Leadbeater's Possum called its distress call. I could not be sure of

Tessa and baby. Possibly the first photograph ever taken of a baby Leadbeater's Possum on its mother's back.

the number of babies in the nest and would not allow the nest to be further disturbed.

On 18 November however, I saw a baby Leadbeater's Possum running around the enclosure. I searched the entire enclosure and probed the nest box but no other young one was to be found anywhere. I concluded that one of Tessa's twins must have died.

Photographs were taken of Tessa with her baby riding on her back on 21 November. This was a great thrill as it was the first of such photographs ever taken.

On December 5, 1978, I saw a baby Leadbeater's poke its head out of Tessa's pouch. I did not pick her up, but judging from her size, I felt she may have been carrying two babies.

For some weeks I observed Tessa closely. Sometimes she was obviously carrying a baby in her pouch, sometimes she carried a baby on her back and sometimes she travelled solo.

On 25 December, 1978, I could resist no longer and I probed Tessa' nest box again. The adults shot out. Tessa had two small babies clinging to her fur. I was obviously wrong about one of the babies having died.

While all the other adults gathered around her, one of the younger adults sprung onto my face and bit me hard on the nose for my trouble. I am sure that in the wild, Leadbeater's will help protect each other in a similar way.

Evicted Females

While the Leadbeater's can be protective of each other, this attitude does not prevail.

I had already discovered that females in particular seem to be evicted by their mothers after a certain age. Tessa had already evicted Gail and The Amazon had also evicted a daughter.

Then 7 September, 1979, old Tessa attacked another of the younger females. While she was biting her daughter on the top of the head and neck, The Gentleman also attacked this daughter. Obviously, female Leadbeater's will sometimes enlist the support of their male mates to evict unwanted daughters.

The poor little female just curled up in a ball making submissive squeals as both parents attacked her.

I quickly caught her and removed her from the enclosure. She was badly bitten and her fur and skin was gone. A wound on her neck was about the size of a one cent piece and another wound on her head was about the size of a two cent coin.

Badly bleeding, I weighed her (149 grams) and placed her in

the laundry to allow her to recover. A few days later, I placed her into the same enclosure as The Amazon's evicted daughter. They did not fight each other.

It became clear that excess females and unmated males must be kept separately from breeding pairs after they reach a certain age in captivity. I realised then, that this issue would present a housing problem for me in the near future.

Tara, Midget And Daughter Rita

Born to Tommy and Tessa, Tara was my first captive-bred Leadbeater's to survive to maturity. Consequently, Tara was very special to me.

Owing to the faulty diet at the time she was born, her twin brother Tiny died very young. Tara also failed to grow to full size. The heaviest she ever weighed was 122 grams. She also had a strangely curled tail.

Midget was also a small animal. Hence his name. He was born to The Gentleman and Tessa in 1977.

In December 1978, Tara and Midget produced twins. Sadly, both twins died when only two weeks out of the pouch.

Tara however, forever worked on nest building and in December 1979, produced a single female. This daughter, whom I called 'Rita', grew well on the improved diet and by July 1980 weighed 160 grams. Interestingly too, Rita did not have a curl in her tail like her mother.

In June 1980, Tara attacked her daughter Rita. Rita being bigger than her mother however, retaliated and for two nights gave her own mother a hiding.

On the third night of the conflict, Midget defended his mate. Together, Tara and Midget then got the better of their daughter and I am quite certain that they would have killed Rita had I not removed her from the enclosure.

Rita, unfortunately escaped from her enclosure some time later and was killed by a cat.

While this was a sad ending, Rita being a second generation captive-bred possum without the physical problems of her parents proved that my diet and breeding program was a success.

Tara, I found dead on the shelf outside her nesting box on 6 March, 1982. Midget died on 18 April, 1985 having reached the fine old age of eleven years. I buried them in the enclosure in which they had spent most of their lives.

Farewell Tara and Midget—I do miss you.

The tiny, delicate, beautiful and endangered Leadbeater's Possum.

5
The Hand Over

B Y 1980, *Des Hackett had a great deal of experience keeping and breeding the Leadbeater's Possum.*

After almost two decades of private and largely unauthorised research, the work of maintaining and breeding the Leadbeater's Possum was set for the next stage. Initially approached by the Frankfurt Zoo, Des realised that to ensure the long-term success of a breeding program was beyond his own resources. Certainly the liberation of captive-bred animals into the wild was beyond Des. This however, had become his ultimate goal.

In January 1981, Des met with the Chairman of the Melbourne Zoological Board, other zoo staff and Fisheries and Wildlife personnel to discuss the practicalities of the zoo continuing the breeding program.

Des provided details of the housing and dietary requirements of the Leadbeater's Possum together with advice about their social and breeding behaviour. The Melbourne Zoo agreed to assume jurisdiction over the colony and the Fisheries and Wildlife Division offered to provide further wild caught animals to add to the breeding program.

A short while later, the Sydney Taronga Park Zoo and the Healesville Sanctuary also became involved in the breeding program. By 1987, the scene was set for the release of captive-bred Leadbeater's Possum into the wild.

Des Hackett's dream was likely to be realised.

Taking Stock

Between 1973 and 1980, a total of twenty-six Leadbeater's Possum had been bred on my premises.

The state of the colony at the end of 1980 consisted of seven males and seventeen females. The number of breeding pairs was three.

Of the twenty-four Leadbeater's kept on my premises by the end of 1979, five were wild ones. The other nineteen consisted of first, second and third generation captive-bred animals.

During the year 1979–1980, I had to strictly curtail further breeding as no more could be kept on my premises. The main problem was that there simply was not enough space in my backyard.

Due to the social structure and fierce nature of the Leadbeater's, they could not be placed in enclosures next to each other. I always had an enclosure of Sugar Gliders between the Leadbeater's.

I also knew that the females selected the male and that both mated males and females would attack and kill other mature females, including their own daughters. Males have also been known to kill each other.

Something had to be done in order to continue the breeding program.

An Approach By The Frankfurt Zoo

On 17 January 1980, two representatives from the Frankfurt Zoo approached me to discuss the availability of the Leadbeater's for their zoo.

Their proposal was that I initially supply two pair. One pair would primarily be for exhibition in their new nocturnal house, while the other pair would be housed in a special enclosure for research and breeding purposes.

They also advised that a similar arrangement be made with Gerald Durrell on one of the Channel Islands (a zoo specifically for breeding endangered animals). Working closely with Durrell, the Frankfurt Zoo felt that they could ensure a successful breeding program in Europe for these rare creatures.

At first I was quite prepared to go to Germany in order to set up suitable enclosures and nesting boxes, and to provide advice about food etc.

I insisted that if I did supply animals that the enclosures would need to meet strict specifications. For one thing, they should be well equipped with plenty of logs for the Leadbeater's to run and leap on so they could stay fit and avoid getting too fat. I also insisted that these logs be stringybark eucalypts so as to provide suitable bark for nest building.

This was most important as the Leadbeater's nest build for much of the year and would not breed without suitable bark logs. Stripping bark is also very important therapy for the captive animals.

If they did not have suitable logs in Germany, they could have them sent from Australia.

I felt willing to co-operate in any way that I could to ensure the survival of the species. Providing that all the requirements were met, I was sure that Frankfurt could breed Leadbeater's.

But then, was there any purpose in letting Frankfurt have the Leadbeater's? What was the attitude of the Fisheries and Wildlife people to the concept of exporting our rare wildlife? Could the Commonwealth provide permits? How would the Leadbeater's cope with twenty-five hours on a plane?

To my mind, the best place for Leadbeater's Possum is in the forest. Breeding them in the Frankfurt Zoo was not likely to have them or their offspring released into the wild.

I decided to get the advice of our own wildlife people before committing myself to the Frankfurt Zoo.

An Agreement Between The Fisheries And Wildlife Department And The Melbourne Zoo

I held several meetings with the Fisheries and Wildlife Department and the management of the Melbourne Zoo during 1980. As a result, an agreement was reached whereby the Zoo would accept most of the Leadbeater's that I had.

The following are extracts from a letter to the Chairman of the Zoological Board of Victoria from the Acting Director of the Victorian Fisheries and Wildlife (January 23, 1981).

"Mr Hackett, under permit from the Division, has kept a colony (of Leadbeater's Possum) at his home for more than a decade. He has, in that time, undertaken considerable personal research on the colony, and has developed a considerable understanding of their dietary needs, conditions necessary for breeding, and social behaviour. Mr Hackett would now like the responsibility for the colony to be transferred to another party, and the bulk of the colony to be relocated…The Division would like your Board to consider being the authority responsible for the colony… [and]…the Division has no objection to your Zoo considering transfer of some of the colony, or future offspring to other zoos, interstate and overseas, once the future of a display colony in Victoria was assured."

The understanding at this stage was that the Frankfurt Zoo and perhaps the Channel Island Zoo would be involved in the breeding program also.

The Fisheries and Wildlife gave the Melbourne Zoo $10,000 as a first payment toward the construction of breeding enclosures specifically designed for the Leadbeater's Possum. The Fisheries also agreed to capture more wild stock to shore up the genetic diversity of the breeding colonies.

On 25 June, 1981, the Deputy Director of the Zoological Board of Victoria wrote to me:

"Following our discussions in the zoo regarding the design and location of the proposed Leadbeater's Possum breeding and holding enclosure, I am now enclosing a copy of our final proposal for your information and possible comment…"

A contract was let and the work on the construction of the enclosures started quite quickly in an area that was off limits to the public. The eight cages were designed to my specifications—ten metres long, sixteen metres wide and over two metres high. I refused to have any reduction in size.

I also insisted that the Leadbeater's were not to have visual contact with those in other cages as they are too fierce and would spend too much time trying to fight.

The Melbourne Zoo would have five breeding pair. There would also be a cage for unattached males and a cage for unattached females.

Between 1981 and 1982, I donated thirteen Leadbeater's Possum to the Melbourne Zoo. These consisted of five mated pairs and three unattached animals. The animals were well selected to give the zoo the best possible opportunity to breed.

The project was an outstanding success and by 1986 the Melbourne Zoo colony numbered thirty individuals.

The Possums That Went To Sydney

Not all of my Leadbeater's Possum were required to establish a colony at the Melbourne Zoo.

Of the animals remaining in my care, most were unmated single females. With the addition of wild caught males, colonies could also be established at Healesville Sanctuary and the Taronga Park Zoo in Sydney.

On 24 September, 1981, I weighed and checked the health of all the animals destined to go to the Taronga Park Zoo. There were three separate colonies, each with great breeding potential.

Colony 1

This colony consisted of four Leadbeater's including Andy, the wild caught male from Camberville, and the female called Nancy. Nancy was a daughter of The Amazon and The Gentleman, both wild caught animals.

With Andy and Nancy were the twin daughters of Nancy born in December 1980. Unrelated to Andy, these young females may in time be able to be bred with him.

Care however, had to be taken to ensure that the group was not kept together to the point of Nancy becoming aggressive towards her daughters as both Andy and Nancy could gang up to kill them.

Colony 2

This family consisted of five animals, a breeding pair and their offspring.

The parents had both been bred from Tessa and The Gentleman and were therefore brother and sister. However, all young were healthy and of good size.

The two female offspring weighed in at 150 and 186 grams, making the larger of the two the biggest female Leadbeater's I have ever bred. No wild caught female has ever reached this weight.

The male, born in November 1980, was also a large animal. At the age of ten months, he already weighed 174 grams. There has never been another male bred in captivity that was so large by this age.

Colony 3

The third colony consisted of a paired male and female together with their eighteen month old daughter. Both adults had been bred in captivity.

The daughter in this group was a very important animal from a breeding point of view as she had the bloodlines of Leadbeater's from three different and widespread areas.

My Last Leadbeater's

I kept only six animals. I kept old Tessa, The Gentleman and The Amazon.

I also kept Tara, Midget and Kathy.

Tara was the daughter of Tommy and Tessa born in 1973. Midget was the son of The Gentleman and Tessa born in 1977. Although related via their mother Tessa, Tara and Midget were a pair who had already produced a set of twins in 1978 and Rita in 1980.

Kathy was born in December 1980. Her mother was The Amazon and her father was Andy, my last wild caught animal from Camberville.

When Tara suddenly died on the 6th of March 1982, I put Kathy and Midget together.

In December 1984, Kate was born. This female had the genes of The Amazon, Andy, Tommy and Tessa, all wild animals captured over a wide range of the Leadbeater's known distribution. She was thus very special.

The Amazon Dies

In the middle of June 1981, I noted one morning that The Amazon was walking around her enclosure holding her head to one side. She was also slow moving. It appeared she had taken a stroke.

She remained in a stabilised condition and was eating well. However, on July 2, 1981, I found her dead, curled up as if asleep. She was in her nest. I gave the body to the Fisheries and Wildlife Division as she was an unusually large female and no doubt of some scientific interest.

Goodbye My Old Friend.

The Gentleman Died of Old Age

In early May 1982, The Gentleman was still strong, eating well and running around the enclosure. Over the next few weeks however, he became slow and obviously weak.

Given that The Gentleman was already 3 or 4 years old at the time of capture in 1971, he may have been 15 years old. He died of extreme old age at 10am on 27 May, 1982.

Goodbye Old Friend.

Tessa Died Pining

Tessa and The Gentleman were very attached to each other and she badly missed The Gentleman. She searched for him for days after his death.

Soon after The Gentleman died, Tessa's eyes began to change to an opaque white colour. By August, Tessa seemed partly blind and she began to lose weight.

Tessa became very slow of movement and by August 25 was very weak. On August 26, Tessa went into a semi-coma and died on the 27 August 1982.

I will always remember you Tessa—Goodbye.

Midget, Kathy and Kate

Midget died on 18 April, 1986, and Kathy died a short while later on 24 June, 1986.

Given that Kate had such an important bloodline and I had no male Leadbeater's Possum from which to breed, I gave Kate to the Healesville Sanctuary.

Reflections

Soon after giving Kate, my last Leadbeater's Possum to Healesville Sanctuary, I began demolishing the enclosures in my backyard.

I found this very sad, but it had to be done. I thought about the many years of keeping these beautiful creatures, developing the feeding and breeding techniques… It was time consuming work and financially costly. But it was a real achievement.

It will seem strange to no longer feed the Leadbeater's Possums; to lay in bed of a night and no longer listen to their strange wild calls. It will be very difficult after having kept them for so long. I will miss them.

But they had to go in order that the breeding of them could continue as a proper project.

I now look back over the long years that I have kept the Leadbeater's Possum and I think of all the work and trouble they gave me. I sometimes wonder if it was all worth while. Will the zoos look after my possums as well as I did? The cost alone was well over $20,000 in food over the years.

While it was a difficult, self-sacrificing and time consuming task, I had the satisfaction of knowing that I was the first person to successfully keep and breed these animals in captivity. I have

experienced the delight of sitting in their enclosures of a night time as these beautiful and curiously shy little marsupials took food out of my hands.

The work to establish Sugar Gliders at Tower Hill was going very well. In February 1981, I placed twelve more young ones into Tower Hill and the Fisheries and Wildlife people tagged them. The latest release brought the number of gliders to eighty-four that had gone to Tower Hill. We also placed a large number of nesting boxes there.

In May, I went to Tower Hill again. With the Fisheries and Wildlife people, I spent a week trapping and tagging the gliders. We trapped over fifty different ones. One female had twin young in her pouch and many other females had already bred.

The Fisheries told me that the young born at Tower Hill were ten to fifteen grams heavier than young of the same age in another study area in Gippsland. Clearly these captive-bred animals were coping well in the wild.

These results gave me great hope for a release program being adopted for my Leadbeater's Possum in a time to come. I'm sure it will all have been worth it.

Annual Reports Reflect Progress

The various zoos were very successful in breeding the Leadbeater's Possum using my original breeding stock and years of experience to assist in the design of enclosures, feeding program and other needs of the animals.

The Healesville Sanctuary Annual Reports stated:

"To provide a sound base to build up stock in other zoos, viable breeding colonies have been established for a number of vulnerable species including Leadbeater's Possum. " (1984–1985).

"Notable species which have continued to breed well include Leadbeater's Possum." (1985–1986)

The 1985–1986 Annual Report of the Melbourne Zoo stated:

"The colony of Leadbeater's Possum continues to flourish. A management plan has been developed for this endemic endangered species, involving relocation of some stock to enhance genetic viability of breeding groups.

Recently sub-adult siblings housed in the same enclosure were separated to remove the possibility of aggressive interactions, a common occurrence amongst maturing female Leadbeater's Possums."

The best news came from the 1986–1987 Healesville Sanctuary Annual Report which stated,

"Of particular importance during the year was the breeding and release programme for the Leadbeater's Possum. This programme represented a unique co-operative breeding effort between the Melbourne Zoo, Taronga Zoo in Sydney and the Healesville Sanctuary.

Having jointly bred a significant number of this threatened species, a release to the wild programme was undertaken by the officers of the Victorian Department of Conservation Forest and Lands.

Initially twelve possums were released and their movements are being monitored by radio-tracking devices.

Early indications are that the programme has been successful although a thorough assessment has not been possible at the time of writing."

One of Des Hackett's Leadbeater's at the Healesville Sancturary.

6
In Summary

HAVING GIVEN *many of the animals names, the following is a brief summary of some of these Leadbeater's Possums according to Des Hackett's notes. While Des was a prolific note-taker, he often failed to date his observations other than birth and death dates. In putting together this book in a diary form, it is the birth and death dates of individual animals that has determined an order for his notes.*

Tommy was the first of Des Hackett's second Leadbeater's Possum colony. Tommy was captured in June 1971 in the Upper Thompson River area. He sired the first Leadbeater's Possum bred in captivity to Tessa in 1972. Tommy died in May 1977 after a physiological change that resembled a change in gender.

The Amazon was captured in August 1971 in the Marysville area. Her first baby to The Gentleman died soon after leaving the nest. She was the dam of Nancy (also to The Gentleman) in 1973, Sahra (to Gus) in 1977 and Kathy (to Andy) in 1980. The Amazon died in July, 1981, after ten years in captivity.

Nixon the Barbarian was captured in August 1971 in the Marysville area. The Barbarian died in March 1974 without any offspring while in captivity.

The Gentleman was also captured in August 1971 with The Amazon and Nixon the Barbarian. He initially sired captive bred Leadbeater's Possum to The Amazon. While the first of these babies died, he also sired Nancy to The Amazon in 1973. Some years later, The Gentleman sired a total of thirteen offspring during his successful mating with Tessa. This included Gus and Gertie in 1976, Gail in 1977 and Midget in 1977. The Gentleman died on 27 May 1982 after almost eleven years in captivity.

Tessa (Mad Nora) *was found by a rally car driver in March 1972 in the Penny Saddle area of the Upper Thompson catchment. She was initially paired up with Nixon but this was not successful due to Nixon's aggressive nature. She later produced the first captive-bred Leadbeater's to Tommy—Tiny and Tara in 1972, and later twins Tony and Toby in 1973. When eventually mated with The Gentleman, Tessa produced a further thirteen offspring. Tessa died one month after her mate, The Gentleman, 27 August, 1982.*

Tiny and Tara *were born in December 1972 to Tommy and Tessa. These twins were the first captive bred Leadbeater's Possums. While Tiny died very young, Tara lived in captivity until 6 March 1982. Tara was mated with Midget and gave birth to twins in 1978. Although these babies died shortly after leaving the pouch, they were full second generation captive-bred Leadbeater's Possum. Tara and Midget produced Rita in 1979.*

Un-named baby—*The first Leadbeater's born to The Amazon and The Gentleman died shortly after leaving the nest in April 1973.*

Tony and Toby *were the second twins of Tommy and Tessa. Born in December 1973, Tony died on 30 April, 1975 of heart failure due to a dietary problem. On an improved diet, Toby lived until 13 September, 1980. Toby was mated with Nancy in 1975 to produce the first of Hackett's second generation captive-bred Leadbeater's.*

Nancy *was born in December 1973 to The Amazon and The Gentleman. She was mated to Toby to produce the first of Hackett's second generation captive-bred Leadbeater's. Nancy went to the Sydney Zoo in 1981.*

Gus and Gertie *were twins born in the spring of 1976 to Tessa and The Gentleman. Gus sired a female (Sahra) to The Amazon before he died on January 4, 1978.*

Gail *was born to The Gentleman and Tessa in April 1977. She was given to Monash University after being evicted from the colony by Tessa in 1978.*

Midget *was born to Tessa and The Gentleman in September 1977. He sired twins to Tara in 1978. These twins died. However in 1979, Midget and Tara produced Rita, a healthy captive-bred second generation Leadbeater's Possum. In 1984, Midget and Kathy produced Kate, Des Hackett's last Leadbeater's Possum. Hackett's last male Leadbeater's Possum, Midget, died in April 1986.*

Leadbeater's No. 16 was captured in the Camberville area in 1977. Given to Des Hackett after being kept at Monash University for two years, this large male did not sire young in captivity and died in 1981.

Sahra was born to Gus and The Amazon in 1977.

Andy was captured in November 1979 in the Camberville area. He sired Kathy to The Amazon in 1980 and was later transferred to the Taronga Park Zoo in 1981.

Rita was born to Tara and Midget in 1979. Although Tara and Midget we both small and Tara had a curl in her tail, Rita, a second generation captive-bred animal had none of these problems. Unfortunately, Rita escaped from her enclosure and was killed by a cat in 1980.

Kathy (sometime called Kelly in Hackett's notes) was born in December 1980 to The Amazon and Andy. Kathy and Midget produced Kate in 1984, Hackett's last Leadbeater's Possum. Kathy died shortly after her mate Midget in 1986.

Steve was captured in the Camberville Junction area in 1982. He only spent a short while with Des Hackett before being sent to Taronga Park Zoo in 1983.

Kate was Des Hackett's last Leadbeater's Possum. Born in 1984 to Kathy and Midget, she was given to the Healesville Sanctuary.

Fred the Sugar Glider deserves a special mention. Although Des bred well over one hundred gliders, it was Fred who started Des Hackett on his quest to breed both gliders and Leadbeater's Possum. Fred was given to Hackett in 1965 and died in 1975.

Flossie from Castlemaine was Des Hackett's first female Sugar Glider. She was acquired in 1967 and breeding of Sugar Gliders began shortly after.

Aussie was possibly Des Hackett's favourite. Those that knew Des Hackett during the late 1970's and early 1980's would have known Aussie. She lived freely within Des Hackett's house and often scampered about his lounge room when Des Hackett had visitors. Des often had Aussie sitting on his shoulder as he worked.

Des Hackett became quite famous for his work with gliders.

7
Successful Gliders

T HE BOX *of notes used to compile this publication predominantly contained material specifically about Des Hackett's work with the Leadbeater's Possum. However, Des was also known for being the first person to successfully breed the Sugar Glider in captivity. Equally as important, Des contributed to the first successful reintroductions of this species into several areas where it had become locally extinct.*

Over a period spanning the best part of three decades, Des bred some 400 gliders. Most of these were reintroduced into various places around the State that had been revegetated.

While Des was frustrated by bureaucracy, he took great pride in his achievements with gliders. The successful release of Sugar Gliders into the wild gave him great hope for similar success with the Leadbeater's Possum.

As Des was a prolific note taker, there is sure to be a box of notes somewhere detailing his work with Sugar Gliders. Using newspaper clippings and copies of letters between Des and various government departments, together with the rare note he included about individual gliders in the 'Leadbeater's box', a few examples of his successful work with these animals are included in this chapter.

A Rare Note About A Glider Called Ken

ON FEBRUARY 14, 1978, I destroyed with ether an old Sugar Glider called Ken.

In November 1976, this male had a large lump on the chest. It was the size of a golf ball cut in half. I had a vet remove the lump. He said it was cancer. The Werribee Vet Clinic confirmed this diagnosis to be true.

I kept this male in an enclosure on his own. Five weeks later, 11 stitches were removed and I placed him back with his colony where he had been the dominant male.

Ken was quickly attacked by another male. This younger animal had taken over as dominant male during Ken's absence.

An obvious difference between the Leadbeater's Possum and Sugar Gliders is the flying membranes of the glider.

The old male did not fight back. He was eventually permitted to sleep with the colony in a subordinate role.

Several months later, Ken had put on a lot of condition. The old male then attacked the young male and regained his place as the dominant male.

In October 1977, the old male developed another lump on his chest. This was on his right side under the arm. It grew rapidly and at about the same time, he lost his dominant position within the colony.

This time, Ken was not permitted to sleep in the nest box with the rest of the colony. He joined several other gliders who had previously been put out of the main nest box, some by Ken himself. He slept with them in another box.

The cancer continued to grow at a rapid rate. It affected his movement so it was time to destroy him.

Petty The Squirrel Glider

During the 1980s, I had played nursemaid to many and varied sick and injured native animals. Some came to me via universities while others were given to me by Fisheries and Wildlife or Forestry Officers.

One of the most interesting animals to be given to me was Petty the Squirrel Glider, one of Victoria's rarest mammals.

Petty was similar in many ways to the Sugar Gliders but much larger. He was found in 1980 lying paralysed after apparently crashing into a power pole near Wangaratta.

The farmer that found Petty passed him on to a Fisheries and Wildlife Officer. This officer then gave Petty to me for rehabilitation.

Petty was part of a PhD study.

Much fuss was made of Petty as he recovered under my care and he became part of a PhD study on Squirrel Gliders. He eventually regained full use of all limbs and was able to run about my house every night. Like clockwork, Petty would retire to a box in the laundry at 7.15 am.

Unfortunately, Petty obviously had brain damage and never fully attained enough balance to glide properly. As he could never be released into the wild, I kept this amazing animal for six years.

Petty died at midnight on May 16, 1986.

Tower Hill—A Great Success

A Challenge

Nestled in a three kilometre-wide volcanic crater near Warrnambool, Victoria is the Tower Hill Game Reserve. Totally cleared in the late 1860s, the three islands within the reserve became the subject of an ambitious experiment in revegetation and wildlife re-colonisation.

Revegetation works began in 1961. As a blue print, the Fisheries and Wildlife Division used an 1855 painting of the area by Viennese artist Eugene von Guerard.

Hundreds of volunteers helped plant 250,000 trees and shrubs. Many bird species returned to Tower Hill as the trees grew. Other animals such as emus, koalas, kangaroos, wombats, bandicoots and echidnas were re-introduced by the Fisheries and Wildlife Division.

As I am the world expert on breeding the Sugar Glider, I was asked to provide gliders for the main 130-hectare island.

The habitat, while still young seemed to contain all the principal dietary requirements for the species. In particular, there were already well-established Manna Gum trees flowering in spring and summer. These complemented the Swamp Gum that flowered in autumn and winter. Black Wattle trees were also well established and these were likely to provide an excellent all year round energy supply by way of sap and gum. All these tree species also attract abundant insects, providing the protein needs of Sugar Gliders.

The experiment had its critics however. Even within the Fisheries and Wildlife Division some said that gliders would not survive. None-the-less, as long as suitable nesting boxes were provided I saw no reason why Sugar Gliders would not do well at Tower Hill.

Releases

In March 1979, the first twenty-six of my Sugar Gliders were released into the Tower Hill Reserve. These animals were selected from my various enclosures and placed together in one large enclosure. In this way they could adjust to each other and to their new nesting boxes before release.

There were twelve males and fourteen females in this first group. Thirteen of the females were six months old and one was two years old. Eleven of the males were six months old and one was three years old. The weight of these animals varied from 140 to 152 grams. All were in excellent condition at the time of release.

A short spotlighting survey by Monash University in July 1979 was not encouraging. No Sugar Gliders were found and the nesting boxes provided could no longer be used by gliders. Many had been taken over by bees while others were already in disrepair. While the report concluded that gliders were still likely to exist, some saw this as evidence that the introduction of gliders into Tower Hill was doomed to failure.

Later spotlighting surveys by local Fisheries and Wildlife Officers indicated that the gliders had settled in well after all. It seems that they had spread out from the initial release sites and were using forms of shelter other than the nesting boxes provided. It was assumed that Sugar Gliders were living in

A night glide at Tower Hill.

abandoned Ringtail Possum drays, decorticating eucalypt bark or even in ground shelter sites. By early January 1980, the Fisheries and Wildlife people believed that the gliders might have even increased by as much as sixty per cent.

During January and February 1980, the population was given an extra boost with the release of a further thirty-four animals supplied by me and the project gained considerable publicity. There were twenty-one males and thirteen females in this second round of releases.

Given that Sugar Gliders are nocturnal and a rarity to the public eye, the Fisheries and Wildlife established feed trees to aid public viewings. A trickle of liquid honey smeared onto certain branches would lure the sweet-toothed gliders into view.

In February 1981, twelve more gliders were released (six males and six females). Thus I had provided a total of seventy-two Sugar Gliders for this project to date.

During May 1981, the Sugar Gliders were again surveyed. Thirty-two animals were captured and tagged. To my mind this was a very positive result.

Still Critics

There were still critics who said that the Sugar Gliders that I had bred and released into the Tower Hill Reserve would not thrive. There were still those who felt that the project was a waste of time and money. Of particular concern to me was that there was no effort made to maintain the nesting boxes that I had provided. Many boxes had been taken over by bees and I became quite sure that this would ultimately doom the project to failure.

I urged the Department to provide more hollows and to maintain those that were available until the young trees developed sufficient natural hollows. In spite of a vigorous campaign on my behalf, the Department was extremely reluctant to put such resources into the project.

In May 1986, I felt forced to write to the Minister of Conservation, Forests and Lands, Joan Kirner, expressing my concerns. She was sympathetic and arranged for the location of the boxes to be mapped and for any boxes occupied by bees to be returned to good order. The critics continued their campaign to discredit the experiment and senior Wildlife Officers in Melbourne remained indifferent to my concerns.

In November 1986, however, a recapture program quickly and finally proved the critics wrong. The habitat at the reserve had improved as trees grew. This allowed Sugar Gliders to spread throughout the reserve as they increased in number.

A mixture of honey and oats was the bait and a trail of diluted honey was laid from the trap to a main stem of the tree as an attraction. Each of fifty-three traps was set every night for four nights and a total of thirty-nine animals were trapped and tagged. There were thirteen males and twenty-six females. Some were trapped more than once.

Success

All animals were in good health. Many of the captured females had young babies in their pouches while others had strongly lactating nipples indicating that more young were in the nests when their mothers were captured.

Three of the females captured in this survey had been tagged during the 1981 survey. One animal re-captured during this survey was already two years of age in 1981. As the average life expectancy of a wild Sugar Glider is only five years, this animal, then over seven years old, proved that the Tower Hill environment was fruitful and that the release program was a success.

The study concluded that the long-term survival rate of released animals was at least equivalent to that of natural wild populations elsewhere. It was also concluded that the population at Tower Hill was at least seventy-nine strong and steadily growing. Many animals were found well away from the original release site indicating that they were successfully populating the entire reserve. The release of captive-bred Sugar Gliders into a revegetated environment was a success. My gliders were doing very well.

Providing more nesting boxes remained a limiting long-term factor and I found the senior Melbourne-based wildlife officers to be devious and smug. They constantly tried to whitewash the disgraceful neglect of the Tower Hill nesting boxes and I considered them to be incompetent. Anything that they had to say or write could not be accepted or believed by me and I swore that for as long as I lived and was able, I would care about the welfare of the Tower Hill gliders. I had provided some eighty boxes at my own expense but maintaining them was beyond me.

With considerable campaigning on my part, the Director of the Department of Conservation, Forests and Lands took over the management of Sugar Gliders at Tower Hill in early 1987. By June that year, a 'wildlife re-establishment project' for Tower Hill was established within the Department's budget and 16 of the 30 nest boxes which had been full of bees were removed and replaced. The future of the Tower Hill gliders looked bright.

The Breeding Cycle

In breeding some 400 Sugar Gliders I have found that they will produce young at the end of July and through August. They nearly always produce twins.

Sometimes, some of the females breed again in January, thus producing four young in one year.

In April and May, both females and males increase their intake of food in order to be in good condition for the winter breeding season.

I have found that gliders should not be trapped in July through to January as disturbing them in this way will sometimes lead to adults killing the pouched young.

February and March are the best months to trap Sugar Gliders. This should be remembered by those studying and trapping these animals in the wild.

Blackburn Lake Reserve—1984 To 1988

A dead Sugar Glider was found by the water's edge of Blackburn Lake in 1974. This was the last evidence of wild Sugar Gliders in the area.

There were plenty of gliders in the area until the 1950s. It was believed that a combination of dwindling habitat, influx of domestic cats and inbreeding within the population resulted in the demise of gliders in the Blackburn area.

On Friday 11 May 1984, with the support of the Blackburn Lake Sanctuary Committee, the Nunawading Council and the Fisheries and Wildlife Department, fourteen of my Sugar Gliders were released into the Blackburn Lake Reserve.

Revegetation works in the area made us confident that the area could support about 100 gliders. A further forty-three gliders were released in the area and a total of eighty breeding boxes were installed.

In 1988, a trapping program was instigated by the Department of Conservation, Forests and Lands to assess the release program. We all expected to find a thriving population of Sugar Gliders within the reserve.

However, only one male Sugar Glider was trapped during the four day period. This baffled us as the sanctuary should have been a virtual supermarket for the gliders in terms of food.

This single male Sugar Glider captured was more than four years old. A tear in the right ear indicated the loss of an ear tag. He was definitely one of the released animals.

He was in excellent condition and weighed a healthy 168 grams. His pectoral scent-making glands were active indicating that he was also sexually active. From this single animal therefore, it was concluded that food was not the reason why Sugar Glider numbers seemed to be low.

However, the study showed that the nesting boxes provided at the time of release had been inhabited by a variety of other animals including rats, Ringtail Possums and birds. It would seem that the Sugar Gliders may have found other, more suitable refuge in the many large old trees outside the reserve. Many such trees could be found on private properties

Page 10 — NUNAWADING GAZETTE, Wednesday March 19, 1986

Sugar gliders make the move to their new bushland homes

SUGAR gliders which have made a successful return to the bushland of Blackburn Lake Reserve will be released experimentally in Yarran Dheran Sanctuary, Mitcham, soon.

Blackburn naturalist Des Hackett, who played a key role in the Blackburn Lake experiment, has bred 22 of the small native squirrel-like animals for the Yarran Dheran project.

The sugar gliders used to live in Blackburn Lake bushland up to the early 1970s but they disappeared because of the decline in their habitat following nearby urban development and the activities of predators like cats.

The attempt to reintroduce sugar gliders began in 1983 with the help of Des Hackett and the Blackburn Lake committee of management member John Wallbrink.

The Fisheries and Wildlife Service co-operated in the pilot program which holds the possibility of returning sugar gliders into parks and reserves in other parts of Victoria.

Des Hackett has bred a total of 22 of the sugar gliders at Blackburn and is hoping Yarran Dheran will prove a new home for them.

Des said at Blackburn Lake the gliders were using special nesting boxes provided high in the trees.

The gliders' name is derived from the fact that they can glide for distances of up to 50 metres.

When leaping they spread their limbs, stretching the skin membrane on either side of their bodies.

They live mainly on the blossom of eucalyptus, banksias, hakeas, and the seeds of wattle.

They like hollow logs for homes and their main enemies are cats, owls, goannas and kookaburras.

DES Hackett and one of the sugar gliders he has bred for release in Yarran Dheran Sanctuary, Mitcham.

adjacent to the reserve and a pair of gliders were sighted in the nearby Kalang Park earlier that year. It could be assumed that the Blackburn gliders may have spread along the Gardiner's Creek Valley.

In spite of the results of this one-off survey, I remained confident that more gliders survived than the single male captured. After all, this male was old but healthy. He was sexually active. Other gliders may simply have been 'trap-shy'.

Yarran Dheran Reserve—1986 To 1989
In March 1986, I introduced twenty-one gliders into the Yarran Dheran Reserve near Mitcham. This was at the request of the Department of Conservation, Forests and Lands.

Gliders lived in the area as recently as the early 1970s, but

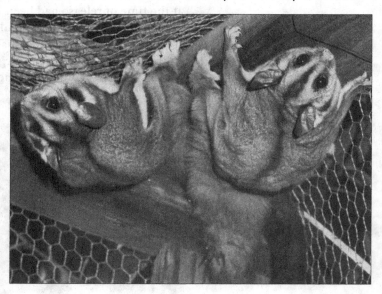

This photo is not upside-down! These two Sugar Gliders are hanging from the roof of the cage.

they disappeared because of the removal of habitat, particularly nesting trees during urban development. Predators like cats would also have had their impact on wild Sugar Glider populations.

This population quickly settled in and grew to at least thirty-one by 1989. This set a precedent for successfully introducing Sugar Gliders into a suburban area. By providing nesting boxes high in trees, gliders might successfully be introduced into other parks and reserves throughout Victoria.

Fairy Island—1988

By 1988 I had decided to close down my breeding program for Sugar Gliders. I agreed to release some of the last of my young animals onto Fairy Island, the smallest island within the Tower Hill Reserve.

While my Sugar Gliders had adapted well on the main island, none had been released onto Fairy Island. I felt that the habitat of the small island was well suited to the gliders.

In March 1988, I provided twenty-two tagged gliders. These animals were not humanised and were most suitable for release. The Department agreed to handfeed the animals for the first few weeks while they settled in. I provided the nesting boxes and the Department promised to provide the necessary maintenance of the boxes.

In **Box No 1** was a single male. He was bred by me in 1986 and at the time of release weighed a healthy 235 grams. He was eighteen months of age and his tag was number 634.

Box No 2 contained a male (660) and a female (656). These twins, bred by me, were also eighteen months old and of similar weight.

Box No 3 also contained one male (608) and one female (609). This set of twins bred by me were only seven month old at the time of release.

Box No 4 contained five gliders—one male and four females. One female was never tagged as she was too difficult to catch and handle. She was given to me by the Department of Conservation, Forests and Lands on 28 September, 1987, after being found in someone's backyard near Geelong. This was not a place one would expect to find Sugar Gliders. Next door to this property resides a woodman who cuts fire wood in the You Yang Ranges. It would appear that this glider came in with a load of wood cut from a felled tree.

The single male (No 620) and one female (621) in this box were bred in captivity by me. The other two females (615 and 618) came to me in January 1988 at about six months of age after their tree was felled. I do not know the location of the tree.

Box No 5 contained one male (661) and two females (662 and 663). The male and one female were bred by me while the other female was wild-caught by the Department in Lang Lang.

Box No 6 contained one male (623) and two females. The male and one female (624) were wild-caught twins. Their tree had been felled but the location was never given to me. The other female (625) was also wild caught as a baby after a tree was felled in the Dandenong Ranges in 1985. She was reared by a wildlife carer and later given to me.

There were six gliders in **Box No 7**—four males and two females. The two females (664 and 666) and one male (665) were about eighteen months old when they were wild caught after a tree was felled in Upwey in December 1986. The other male (604) was reared by a woman after a tree was felled in Vermont in December 1985. I called this male Brad and he was the dominant male in this group.

The other two males (605 and 606) were Brad's sons bred from the wild females.

Earlier critics of the release program were concerned about inbreeding and that genetically my gliders were not the same as the original type in the area. However, mixing animals from vastly different areas was a logical thing. They would breed and adapt to their new wild conditions as the habitat developed.

Sugar Gliders have been successfully re-introduced to many places throughout Victoria.

Organ Pipes National Park—1990 To 1996

I have found that in captivity, Sugar Gliders will eat the blossom of eucalypts, banksias and bottle-brush, but only the fully matured blossoms. They do not eat the blossom of any wattle but when given the seed pods of Cootamundra, Silver, Ovens and Black Wattle, the gliders open the pods and nibble bits of the pods where the seed is located. I believe that the Sugar Glider will eat the seed of most species of acacia.

The resin produced by wattles is very important to the Sugar Glider as is the gum of certain eucalypts.

I also found that my captive Sugar Gliders would eat crickets,

Gliders were found to eat a wide variety of insects.

moths, grasshoppers, locusts, huntsman spiders, wood grubs, preying mantis and cicadas. Gliders no doubt play an important role in controlling such insects in the wild.

When the Friends of the Organ Pipes National Park, an eighty-five hectare reserve near Keilor, found that their revegetation works were being threatened by an infestation of insects, it was decided to introduce Sugar Gliders to help restore the balance.

At the turn of the century, Sugar Gliders were still scattered throughout the area. But, as the land was cleared for agriculture, the gliders disappeared. In 1988, forty of my last Sugar Gliders were re-introduced into the Park to eat the parasites. Several more were introduced from Toolern Vale, north-west of Melbourne. These were wild caught by the Department of Conservation, Forests and Lands.

By 1996, the Sugar Glider population was doing well, having grown to more than 100 animals.

My Last Gliders

After over thirty years of working with Sugar Gliders, I had grown tired of dealing with government departments. I estimate that the breeding program has cost me more than $50,000 and I have had no government assistance for my work.

After the release of the Organ Pipes and Fairy Island gliders, I decided to stop breeding Sugar Gliders.

All that remained in the 19 large cages in my backyard were Aussie, a six year old pet and ten other gliders who were too old to release. I also kept some old Leadbeater's Possum.

Shortly after, I set about dismantling the cages in my backyard.

Some of Des Hackett's last Sugar Gliders.

Des Hackett with Aussie the Sugar Glider.
It is intersting to note that Des was charged for keeping wildlife without a permit shortly after releasing his last Sugar Gliders. He obviously made himself unpopular with the Department of Conservation, Forests and Lands for pushing a release program for Leadbeater's Possum.

8
Zoos Face A Dilemma
1984–1992

IN 1985, *the Healesville Sanctuary reported that:*

"...the species breeding programme continued this year with successful breeding and rearing of a number of small marsupials...[and]...notable species which have continued to breed well are the Brush-tailed Bettong, Ground Cuscus, Leadbeater's Possum, Squirrel Glider, Grey Dorcopsis Wallaby and the Kowarc."

In the same year, the Melbourne Zoo reported that:

"The colony of Leadbeater's Possum continues to flourish. A management plan has been developed for this endemic endangered species involving relocation of some stock to enhance genetic viability of breeding groups."

The 1985/1986 Melbourne Zoo's Annual Report however, alluded to a pending dilemma.

"Recently sub-adult siblings housed in the same enclosure were separated to remove the possibility of aggressive interactions, a common occurrence amongst maturing female Leadbeater's Possum."

By 1987, the issue of aggressive behaviour between Leadbeater's

Possum, and the problem of overcrowding had become an obvious concern to zoos. The Melbourne Zoo's 1986/1987 Annual Report stated that:

"The Leadbeater's Possum breeding facility reached capacity during the year as the result of eight young being born and another five carried in the pouches of three females...

The likelihood of maturing female Leadbeater's Possum (Gymnobelideus leadbeateri) being subjected to aggression from older, breeding females is well known. It is only the expertise of the animal keepers which can reduce the levels of aggression, thereby minimising the number of fatalities."

Des Hackett began a campaign of phone calls and letter writing to have excess Leadbeater's Possum released into the wild. He soon found that his dream was not shared by all others.

The zoos were quite keen on a release program. However, the Victorian Wildlife Authority, which by this time had been amalgamated with the Forestry Service, conducted only one single release project for Leadbeater's Possum. This failed.

Based on the results of the failed release effort, further release of captive-bred Leadbeater's Possum became a low priority. This left the zoos with the problem of surplus animals.

Des made himself unpopular. He publicised that an endangered species was breeding well in captivity, indeed to the point whereby they "were dying of stress due to overcrowding". He exposed the fact that nothing was being done to release the endangered species into the wild.

Too Many Possums—1984

IN NOVEMBER 1984, I went to the Melbourne Zoo to see how my Leadbeater's were going.

The breeding program had been a great success. However, the Chief Officer of Animal Husbandry told me that they already had problems with surplus numbers of Leadbeater's. The zoo, he said, was negotiating with the Frankfurt and London Zoos to take some of the surplus animals.

Ample space was available for more enclosures, but the zoo did not have the funds to build them. There was room for only five pairs.

I was particularly concerned that small wire cages had been built inside the main enclosures to keep the adult Leadbeater's apart. I knew this was likely to result in considerable stress as the animals became more aggressive toward each other. Deaths had already occurred.

I wrote to the Taronga Park Zoo and found that they also had problems with surplus animals. They indicated that they were considering an end to breeding to avoid stress and fighting. However, they also knew that breeding would be difficult to start again after bonded pairs were separated or as breeding animals got too old.

I wrote letters to the Director of the Fisheries and Wildlife Division, the Minister for Conservation and Environment and numerous other bureaucrats. I pushed for a release program for the excess Leadbeater's. It simply did not make sense for Leadbeater's bred in zoos to die of stress from overcrowding while they remained endangered in the wild.

I did not spend so many years developing a breeding program to see my possums die like that in zoos.

The zoos were all prepared to release excess animals and supported my enthusiasm for a release program.

A Distribution Plan For Leadbeater's—1985

By February 1985, the zoos and the Victorian Department of Conservation, Forests and Lands were taking action.

A distribution plan for the species was being developed so that surplus animals would be sent to other zoos throughout the world.

While this plan would deal with the problem of excess animals in the short term, it was likely to create the same problem in many more zoos within a short time. My push to have this endangered animal released into the wild was being ignored by the wildlife agency.

I began to question the purpose of breeding animals in zoos but was constantly told that establishing more captive colonies would ensure against the possibility of failure in any one particular colony. Moving animals between zoos would also facilitate proper genetic management and stop in-breeding within the overall breeding program.

I was assured that in time, this strategy would ultimately provide additional healthy animals to release into the wild.

I continued to write letters of concern and pushed for action on the part of the Department of Conservation, Forests and Lands to instigate a release program.

Interest From Other Zoos—1986

The Taronga Park Zoo sent a form letter to several zoos throughout the world inviting them to accept surplus Leadbeater's Possum.

The letter from the Assistant Director, dated 15 of January 1986 stated:

"This species (Leadbeater's Possum) which until recently was thought to be extinct, was rediscovered in the 60s when a modest population was found to exist in mountain forests in eastern Victoria. A captive breeding programme has been initiated mainly through the efforts of Healesville Sanctuary and, to date, has been met with such success that quite considerable numbers of animals are available to join what we hope will be a well-formulated species management programme.

The stage has arrived where these animals can, under certain circumstances, be made available to participating zoos overseas and I have approached you directly to see if you have any interest in this particular species. I have included some brief details on the species, which is a fantastic animal to be exhibited in any nocturnal house. The management and housing requirements are fairly straightforward..."

There was no mention of the problems of stress due to overcrowding or fighting among adults. There was no mention of a release program. I continued to ask why our wildlife should be sent overseas when they were still endangered in the wild.

The General Curator of Mammals at the San Diego Zoo was the first to reply to Taronga Park.

"You have no idea how I appreciate your approaching us relative to this extremely rare marsupial. I would be thrilled to participate in the management program."

The Assistant Director of The Brookfield Zoo was quick to follow.

"It's nice to know that captive propagation efforts have had a positive influence on the species overall...We would be happy to participate. We are preparing to renovate our Australian building and could incorporate display space for the species."

By early February, the Director of Live Collections at the Toronto Zoo responded.

"We would be delighted to participate in the management programme for the Leadbeater's Possum."

A short while later the Director of the Zoological Research Department at the Washington Zoo also expressed interest in the Leadbeater's Possum.

"I am quite excited to hear of the success of the breeding program. I presume that these animals have descended from a colony donated to the Melbourne Zoo a few years back? I remember visiting this colony during my visit in 1983. We are indeed interested in obtaining Gymnobelideus."

Other zoos including the Frankfurt Zoo, the Metro Zoo in Canada and the London Zoo also expressed an interest in accepting the Leadbeater's Possum.

My concern about breeding more Leadbeater's just for the sake of it grew. I was particularly concerned that laws controlling zoos in the USA are different to those of Australia. In the USA, zoos may and do sell surplus animals to the public.

I have not spent many years perfecting a way to breed these rare possums just so that they can be exploited for money overseas. I was assured that all Leadbeater's exported to overseas zoos and their offspring would remain the property of the

Australian donating zoo. But, I do not believe such a condition could be applied. I could see a time when Leadbeater's Possum would be sold overseas while they continue to be endangered in the wild.

I became even more determined to see this endangered animal released into the wild.

The First Release—1987

Finally, to alleviate overcrowding of Leadbeater's Possum, the Zoological Board of Victoria suggested the possibility of releasing some animals into the wild. The Department of Conservation, Forests and Lands agreed to undertake such a program on a trial basis only.

Direct descendants of The Gentleman and Tessa that had been housed at Melbourne Zoo and Healesville Sanctuary were made available for the release program. The Taronga Park Zoo provided descendants of Nancy and Andy for the program.

In 1987, a total of twelve (four females and eight males) were released in the Central Highlands of Victoria. Four sites were chosen for the release, two in the Toolangi State Forest and two in the Marysville State Forest.

Research had already shown that Leadbeater's Possum are aggressive to strange individuals of their own kind and will vigorously defend their territory. Therefore the release sites were chosen in the areas that did not contain hollow trees, but were considered suitable in terms of other known habitat requirements. It was assumed that because these areas had no suitable nesting sites, wild populations of the species would not occur.

About two days after release of the captive-bred animals, wild Leadbeater's Possum appeared, harassed the released animals, ate their food and took up residence in the nest boxes.

Four of the released animals had been fitted with radio transmitters and tracking of these animals showed that they stayed in the general vicinity of the release sites using a variety of other shelters.

One animal was recaptured twenty days after release and was found not to have lost weight. After a period of two months however, no released animals could be located in the vicinity of the release sites although wild Leadbeater's continued to inhabit these areas now that nesting boxes were available.

The Department of Conservation, Forests and Lands insisted

that they had made efforts to find other suitable release sites with no success. However, they admitted that the release of captive-bred Leadbeater's Possum was not a high priority in their management of the species.

I obviously questioned the choice of release sites. I argued that there was a lot of forest out there where Leadbeater's no longer exist. Logging and land clearing for agriculture has isolated many pockets of forest and there are plenty of places where wild Leadbeater's can no longer reach.

I felt that this release program was successful. At least one animal was found without losing any weight over a long period, even with competition from wild possums. That they could not be found at the end of the trial does not mean that they did not survive. They may have moved on and found other areas to live. Did we not learn anything from the Sugar Glider experience?

My persistent phone calls and numerous letters continued to fall on deaf ears month after month, year after year. Meanwhile, my possums in the zoos continued to breed for no reason but for scientific curiosity and public display. I questioned the value of zoos all together.

A Population Crisis—1989

By 1989, the situation in the zoos had become chronic. The Melbourne Zoo alone had bred some forty-two Leadbeater's Possum (nineteen males and twenty-three females) since I gave them the initial thirteen animals in 1981.

In the eight years, twenty-two Leadbeater's had died of various causes, some no doubt related to stress and overcrowding. Healesville Sanctuary and Taronga Park Zoo were experiencing similar problems.

New colonies had been established in overseas zoos supplied by the Melbourne Zoo, Healesville Sanctuary and the Sydney Taronga Park Zoo. Exporting animals to expand the captive breeding populations was in accordance with the species management plan but releasing animals into the wild was no longer on the agenda.

I continued to lobby for further releases only to be told that this was not a priority of the Department of Conservation. The zoos had no option but to allow excess animals to die in captivity, continue to export excess animals or to stop breeding.

By this stage I was making myself very unpopular with the Department of Conservation. I found that to get any information about their plans for my Leadbeater's Possum, I had to resort to formally applying via the Freedom of Information Act. For this privilege of finding out about my possums I had to pay a fee.

I often passed information on to the media so that the pressure to develop a release program continued. But still nothing was done. I was just constantly told that the Leadbeater's Possum was not a priority of the Department and that no money was available for further release programs.

I was sure that the zoos would soon have to kill older and excess Leadbeater's to ensure a young breeding colony. In my opinion, the Victorian Fisheries and Wildlife people had abandoned the zoos and had left them with a great dilemma. The Fisheries and Wildlife certainly abandoned the Leadbeater's Possum.

A Waste Of A Lifetime?—1992

In October 1992, I visited the London Zoo and inspected the Leadbeater's Possum on display there.

There were eight females and just one male possum. All were in good health, but due to the age of the male, breeding had ceased.

The London Zoo told me that they wanted to exchange animals with Brookfield Zoo in the USA but were unable to do so because the Australian Government would not allow it. They admitted that there was no real conservation purpose in them keeping Leadbeater's.

Upon return to Australia, I sought information from the Australian zoos keeping Leadbeater's. Sydney Zoo was still breeding them but to no purpose other than for public display in their nocturnal house.

Healesville Sanctuary also bred and displayed Leadbeater's Possum in their nocturnal house. However, they also questioned the value of keeping the animals given the lack of a release program.

The Melbourne Zoo did not display Leadbeater's Possum, although a limited level of breeding continued.

The Perth Zoo had received two Leadbeater's Possum from Melbourne Zoo. I was told that they were a male called Squirrel and a female called Tag. I had given these animals to the Melbourne Zoo in 1982. They had not bred and the zoo had no intention of breeding. In fact, the Perth Zoo told me that if they were to breed, the offspring would be disposed of.

As all Leadbeater's that are kept in zoos both here and overseas are the result of my initial breeding work, I seriously questioned my efforts. As nothing was being done to release captive-bred animals into the wild, I began to think that I had wasted my time.

I quote from the letter sent to me by the Taronga Park Zoo Curator of mammals in 1986:

"… Already we have far exceeded our holding capacity and are faced with the decision to stop breeding until there is some relief in sight.

It would be sad and perhaps irresponsible of us not to undertake a rehabilitation and wild-release of surplus animals when, thanks to your early efforts, they are so easily bred in captivity and yet so rare in the wild…"

Des with volunteers at the Hackett Tree.

9
The Hackett Tree

TIMBER HARVESTING *in the Central Highland Forests of Victoria had been relatively low key since the devastating bushfires of 1939. This combined with the many hollows left by the 1939 fires was the very reason why the areas around Noojee, Powelltown and Marysville had become the stronghold of the Leadbeater's Possum.*

In 1990 however, the Department of Conservation, Forests and Lands (now the Department of Sustainability and the Environment) announced plans to dramatically intensify logging operations in the Regions 'regrowth forests'. This threatened the recent recovery of Leadbeater's Possum populations.

As the discovery of any Leadbeater's Possum in a patch of forest resulted in a 'no-go-zone' for the timber industry, releasing captive-bred animals was certainly unlikely.

By this time, Des Hackett had become quite a thorn in the side of the Department because of his tenacious efforts to protect the Leadbeater's Possum. He continued to push for a release program for zoo-bred Leadbeater's. This resulted in a level of professional arrogance on behalf of some 'qualified' wildlife scientists who resented being told what to do by an unqualified naturalist.

To shut him up, the Department even charged Des Hackett for 'harbouring wildlife without a permit'. Ironically, the wildlife in Des Hackett's possession were mainly old Sugar Gliders remaining from his earlier release work with the Department and he was still unofficially receiving gliders orphaned and injured during logging operations for rehabilitation from sympathetic departmental staff. Yet, he now faced prosecution.

In 1991, the environment movement used the plight of the Leadbeater's Possum to draw public attention to the Department's plan to intensify logging operations within the Central Highland Forests. Des Hackett, who to this point had received little public acknowledgement for his work with Leadbeater's, suddenly found himself the centre of attention.

A boardwalk was constructed to a tree named in recognition of Des Hackett. Displays about his work were mounted in a small shelter near the 'Hackett Tree' where visitors could sit and wait for a family of Leadbeater's to emerge from a hollow at dusk. A book was also published by the Australian Wildlife Protection Council about his work and the forestry issues in the region.

Unfortunately, even this tribute ended in disaster, adding to Des Hackett's despair for the future of the Leadbeater's Possum.

Volunteers working at the Hackett Tree.

A Giant Tree

A FEW KILOMETRES beyond Powelltown in the Central Highland stands a magnificent Mountain Ash.

Scarred but spared by the 1939 bushfires and miraculously left after a century of logging, this lone giant stands as a monument of what once was.

I discovered the tree many years ago while I searched for and found one of the earliest known colonies of Leadbeater's Possum.

During the winter of 1991, members of the Australian Wildlife Protection Council, the Environmental Youth Alliance, the Australian Conservation Foundation, the Wilderness Society and the Upper Yarra Conservation Society constructed a boardwalk and viewing platform to the tree.

Over 400 people were involved in the construction of the boardwalk. Almost every weekend for over three months, teams

Getting to the Hackett Tree.

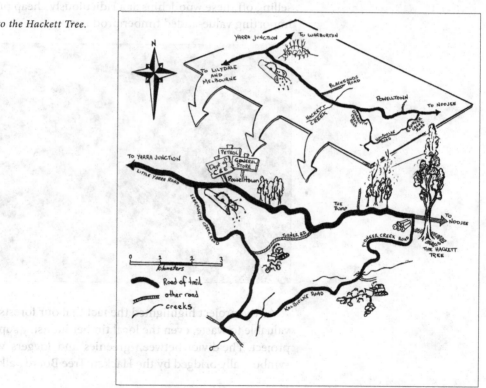

of volunteers made their way to the Central Highland Forests to work on the project.

The display included information about my work with the Leadbeater's Possum. A viewing platform was designed to allow visitors to sit and watch Leadbeater's emerge from a hollow about one third of the way up the ninety metre tree.

As the tree is just one kilometre from a major tourist road, it attracted hundreds of visitors. The Hackett Tree Project therefore provided a readily accessible, yet not too intrusive way for people to observe and learn about the relationship between plants and animals—in this case the reliance of the Leadbeater's Possum on large hollow trees.

Made of locally grown and sawn hardwood, the boardwalk demonstrated that Australia did not need to import timber products such as tropical rainforest timbers or old growth cedar weatherboards. At the time, thirteen per cent of the nation's deficit was a direct result of our timber trade imbalance. We were (and still are), wood-chipping eighty per cent of the trees felled in the Central Highland Forests around the Hackett Tree, selling off these woodchips at a ridiculously cheap price while importing value-added timber products.

As the project highlighted the fact that our forests are too valuable to waste, even the local timber industry supported the project. The divide between 'greenies' and 'loggers' was being symbolically bridged by the Hackett Tree Boardwalk.

A Great Thrill

I had spent hours, days and weeks on end sitting under the Hackett Tree studying the Leadbeater's Possum. It was a great thrill to be acknowledged by so many people in a practical way.

In the days when I visited the tree, there was only a track leading to the area where the tree stands. I had to bush-bash the last 200 metres to get to it.

This forest is usually very wet, and I was often covered in leaches after spending time studying the Leadbeater's.

It was wonderful to share the experience of watching the Leadbeater's emerge from their hollow. It was quite luxurious to have a timber boardwalk to get to the tree, a rainproof viewing platform and a seat upon which to sit while waiting for the animals to do their thing at dusk.

Visitors did not even have to concern themselves with leaches as they were off the ground at all times.

The greatest thrill came in November 1991 when the Hackett Tree Boardwalk was officially opened by Channel Nine's weatherman and Australian Conservation Foundation Councillor, Rob Gell. Over 200 local school children hammered in the last of the nails into the boardwalk on the day of the launch.

Representatives of the Conservation Department were there along with the various environment groups associated with the project. Even local timber workers helped swell the crowd to 400 people.

Everyone understood the environmental and political points being made by the project and the need to manage our forests better.

To the delight of everyone, particularly the kids, the climax of the opening came when a group of people dressed as singing animals emerged from the forest. Everyone joined in when Vox Bandicoot, an environmental theatre company, ended the official proceedings with their own toe-tapping song written especially for the event called 'Don't Hackett the Trees'.

History Torched

On January 8, 1992, some bastard torched my tree.

The boardwalk was built so that people from all over the world could visit the tree and see the endangered Leadbeater's Possum in its natural habitat. The project had brought many people from many different viewpoints together.

Environmentalists built the boardwalk, but the project also had strong support from the local timber industry. To demonstrate that the greenies and loggers could work and think together, one local sawmiller even donated the timber used for the project.

But some idiot did not have the brains to understand that. On a day of total fire ban, the bastard poured diesel into a hollow near the base of the tree and set fire to it.

Hollow, the tree soon acted like a giant chimney. The flames moved up the inside of the tree and smoke bellowed up out of the top of the tree.

The Leadbeater's and other wildlife inside the tree were killed.

I was obviously very angry and upset. The newspaper reports at the time quoted me as saying that the bastard responsible needed shooting.

I do not remember saying that, but I may have as I was understandably upset. I also felt responsible in some ways. I should never have told people about the tree in the first place. I felt like giving up working for wildlife all together.

The Hackett Tree Survives

Fortunately a tourist came across the fire in the Hackett Tree shortly after the arsonist left the scene. The local Country Fire Authority were called in and the fire was put out.

If it were not for the speedy actions of the tourist and the CFA volunteers, the situation could have been devastating. Had it been a windy day and had the fire escaped from the tree, the whole forest could have gone up in smoke. The people of Noojee and Powelltown could have been trapped like they were in 1939.

Of concern to the Department of Conservation and Environment after the fire was that the tree would fall over.

At first it was thought that the Hackett Tree would have to be felled following the fire. But everyone rallied to save the tree. The media, the various environment groups and the local timber industry all lobbied for the tree to be left alone.

The CSIRO and Conservation Department experts assessed the tree and determined that it would survive. It was badly damaged with half of the trunk for over one third of the way up burnt away. Even some of the roots had smouldered away after the actual fire was put out. But the Hackett Tree would survive.

The tree is exactly one kilometre up Pioneer Creek Road from the main road to Noojee past Powelltown. The top can still be seen from the road (on the left driving up). It may remain standing for another hundred years. However, it will fall down one day and the fire, while not killing the tree, will have made that day come sooner.

Inspection shows tree is still structurally sound

Historic Hackett Tree to survive the 'chop'

By LERISSE SMITH

THE historic Hackett Tree which vandals set alight two weeks ago will not be cut down.

Officers from the Department of Conservation and Environment together with an expert from Burnley Gardens, declared the tree structurally sound after an inspection last Thursday. They used electronic equipment to find not much damage had been done internally.

The Mountain Ash was discovered by and named after naturalist Mr Des Hackett 25 years ago.

He told the *Express* he was 'very relieved' to hear the tree would survive.

"I was convinced the tree would not die, but survive," he said.

The Conservation and Environment department forestry officer, Mr Peter McHugh, said the inspection of the tree found it was in better condition than expected.

Boardwalk

"We're happy and pleased that not much damage was done internally, however, the boardwalk might have to be modified," he said.

The Forest Protection Society deplored the vandalism act against the tree and Healesville FPS branch president, Mrs Jan Culton said the Hackett Tree was an appropriate monument to the dedication of one man's work towards the conservation of the Leadbeater possum.

"It is disgraceful that this majestic old tree could be deliberately burnt. Burning it was a very disrespectful act not to mention the potential danger of starting a bushfire," she said.

"The Hackett Tree is an example of how, through proper management, the Central H lands multiple-use ests can offer a variety of values to community ranging f environmentally frie forest products thro to wildlife experier heritage and educatio

Consequently, the boardwalk was closed by the Department. All the signage has been removed so as not to encourage the general public to visit the tree. Those that know where it is may still visit the tree, but they do so at their own risk.

In the meantime, the Hackett Tree will be left alone. I like to think that Leadbeater's Possum may recolonise the upper parts of the tree one day. Who knows, the Department of Conservation and the zoos may even get their act together and release some of their captive-bred Leadbeater's into the area.

Wouldn't that be nice.

A logging coupe in the Central Highlands.

10
The Final Chapter?

THE FINAL *chapter of this book has not yet been written. That's right, this book is not yet complete.*

How do you feel about having read an unfinished book? If you paid good money for this 'incomplete' book, you have a right to feel swindled. However, just think how Des Hackett felt toward the end of his life.

Des dedicated almost thirty years of his life to wildlife conservation and made an enormous academic contribution to the capacity of zoos around the world to care for and breed endangered marsupials. While zoos still use Des Hackett's formulae for feeding possums and gliders, he received precious little recognition.

More importantly, Des handed over successfully breeding colonies of a species that he had dragged back from the edge of extinction, yet was given no say in their future.

Little wonder that Des Hackett spent the later years of his life as a disgruntled recluse. He wrote letter after letter to Minister after Minister asking for action to be taken to protect the Leadbeater's Possum. He desperately wanted, within his lifetime, to see the animals that he had bred, released into the wild.

Unfortunately, nothing has been done to liberate captive-bred Leadbeater's. Even though most zoos were experiencing population explosions of Leadbeater's Possum; even though the animals were killing each other for want of space in captivity; and even though Leadbeater's remained endangered in the wild; no release program has been instigated.

Since Des Hackett died, things have got worse. Zoos were

faced with the dilemma of having over-bred the Leadbeater's but were not able to release excess stock. There are now no breeding programs and the captive colonies have died out.

In 1997, when this book was started, there were active breeding programs in zoos throughout the world. By 2005, when the draft of this book was completed, there were just two individual Leadbeater's left at Healesville Sanctuary and four at the Metro Zoo in Toronto Canada.

By the time this book went to print in 2006, the four Canadian Leadbeater's Possum had also died.

Is it too difficult to secure the existence of the Leadbeater's Possum and a viable, sustainable forest industry?

In the wild, the Leadbeater's Possum remains endangered. With most of its natural range being within forests zoned for 'timber production', the future of the Leadbeater's Possum is far from secure.

Ironically, most of the forests in which the Leadbeater's Possum can be found are relatively young forests. Regrown since the 1939 bushfires, up to 80% of the trees felled from these forests are simply wood-chipped for paper production. As the old nesting trees are felled or naturally degenerate, the wild population of Leadbeater's Possum is on the decline.

All this questions the function of zoos in terms of keeping and breeding endangered species. All this questions the capacity of Australian Government Wildlife Agencies to conserve our unique wildlife.

To complete this final Chapter, Zoos Victoria, the Victorian

Department of Sustainability and Environment and the Victorian Association of Forest Industies were invited to provide guest essays as a right of reply to this ironic situation.

Each of these potential contributors play important roles in the future of the Leadbeater's Possum. Each has expressed enthusiasm for this publication and the opportunity to provide their perspective on why captive-bred Leadbeater's were never released and how best to manage wild populations.

The Leadbeater's Possum Has Friends

To encourage constructive debate about the future management of the Leadbeater's Possum, an enthusiastic group of individuals have formed the Friends of the Leadbeater's Possum. *This new group includes environmentalists, naturalists, educators, researchers and zoo keepers.*

As a group, they have enthusiastically supported this publication and with their help we may see a second edition of this book. The final chapter should be entitled 'Where To From Here' and should include contributions from those organisations and government authorities responsible for the future of the endangered Leadbeater's Possum.

Below is a list of other groups and organisations who have an interest in this issue and/or have endorsed this publication. You can assist their conservation efforts by becoming a member or sending a donation.

Leadbeater's Possum—the faunal emblem of the State of Victoria—is at risk.

Australian Wildlife Protection Council
247 Flinders Lane
Melbourne VIC 3000

Friends of the Leadbeater's Possum
P.O. Box 1175
Healesville VIC 3777

Upper Yarra Conservation Society
P.O. Box 350
Yarra Junction VIC 3797

Warburton Advancement League
P.O. Box 8
Warburton VIC 3799